Evil in Our Midst

Protecting Children from Sexual Predators

SHARON W. DOTY

Arpeggias, LLC

TULSA, OKLAHOMA

Evil in Our Midst
Protecting Children from Sexual Predators

MMDK Consulting, LLC
Arpeggias, LLC
1611 S. Utica, #309
Tulsa, OK 74104
Info@arpeggias.com
http://www.arpeggias.com

©2010 by Arpeggias, LLC

ISBNs 978-0-9770953-3-9

Library of Congress Control Number: 2010920607

Printed in Canada

DEDICATION

*To Leslie Zieren and Saham Tafreshi for their
continuing expressions of love, generosity,
and unwavering support. Because of your
selflessness and genuine concern for others the
world is a better place.*

CONTENTS

	Dedication	iii
	Acknowledgment	vii
CHAPTER 1	Transforming the Approach	1
CHAPTER 2	Discover a Compelling Interest	9
CHAPTER 3	Evil Speaks for Itself	23
CHAPTER 4	Identifying Potential Predators	29
CHAPTER 5	PRB #1: Always Isolated and Alone	35
CHAPTER 6	PRB #2: Gifts That are not "Gifts"	39
CHAPTER 7	PRB #3: Too Much Touching	45
CHAPTER 8	PRB #4: Inappropriately Indulging Children	53
CHAPTER 9	PRB #5: "No Rules" Apply	57
CHAPTER 10	PRB #6: Going it Alone	63
CHAPTER 11	PRB #7: Being "the Answer"	67
CHAPTER 12	PRB #8: Cultivating Relationships with Children	73
CHAPTER 13	PRB #9: Sexual Language and Adult Materials	77
CHAPTER 14	PRB #10: Collecting Memorabilia	81

CHAPTER 15   The Internet: Different and   85
              Similar Behaviors

CHAPTER 16   OPEN Interactions   89

CHAPTER 17   Organizational Responsibility   97

CHAPTER 18   Code of Conduct   105

CHAPTER 19   Creating & Monitoring Access   111

CHAPTER 20   Monitor the Environment   115

CHAPTER 21   Using the Sex Offender Registry   117

CHAPTER 22   Communicate and Act   123

CHAPTER 23   Continuing to Learn   133

CHAPTER 24   Strengthening Children   137

CHAPTER 25   How to Know a Sex Offender   145
              is Now Safe

CHAPTER 26   Turning the Tide of Child   149
              Sexual Abuse Prevention —
              the "Big Picture"

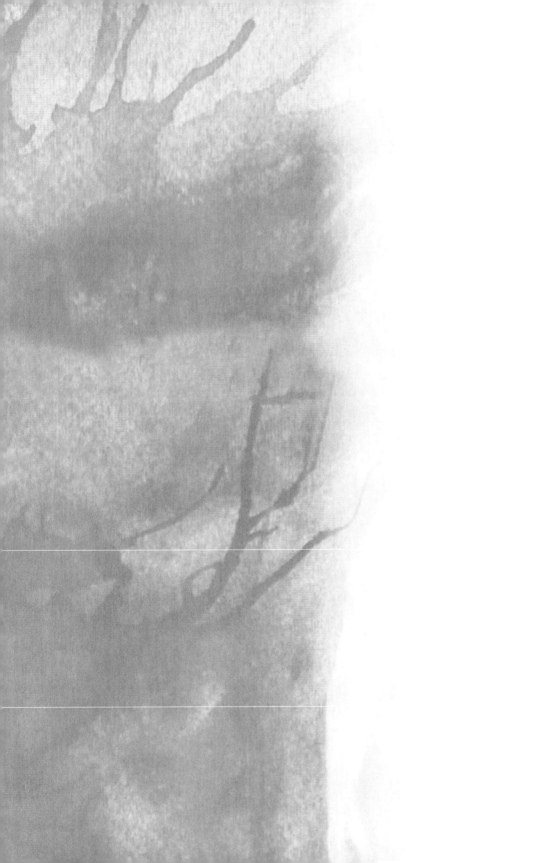

ACKNOWLEDGMENTS

As with many authors I would be remiss if I did not stop to acknowledge the many people whose support has made this book possible. Among those deserving mention are David Finkelhor, Barbara Bonner, Phyllis Willerscheidt, Fr. Steven Rossetti, Jeff Lester, Michael Bemi, the board of National Catholic Risk Retention Group, Inc., and The AGOS Group, LLC for their commitment to sponsoring and supporting the research necessary to develop this approach to the issue of child sexual abuse prevention. Elizabeth Jackson's brilliant art, which graces the cover of this book, is a testament to her amazing commitment to the subject matter and her vision of the evil that molests children. Others who have provided relentless support and encouragement include my editor Tomme Fent, David Holden, Alinda Jones, Kim Justilian, Leslie Zieren, Mary Rounds, my husband, Ned, and my children, Shannon, Ted, and Erica. In addition, the never ending commitment of Diane White and Jessica Powell at Emerge Interactive Media to promoting the ideas in this book cannot be measured. Finally, I acknowledge the commitment of professionals in the field of child sexual abuse prevention and treatment. Their unwavering dedication to find solutions to these problems in society continues to inspire me to find ways to make this information available to the adults in our communities.

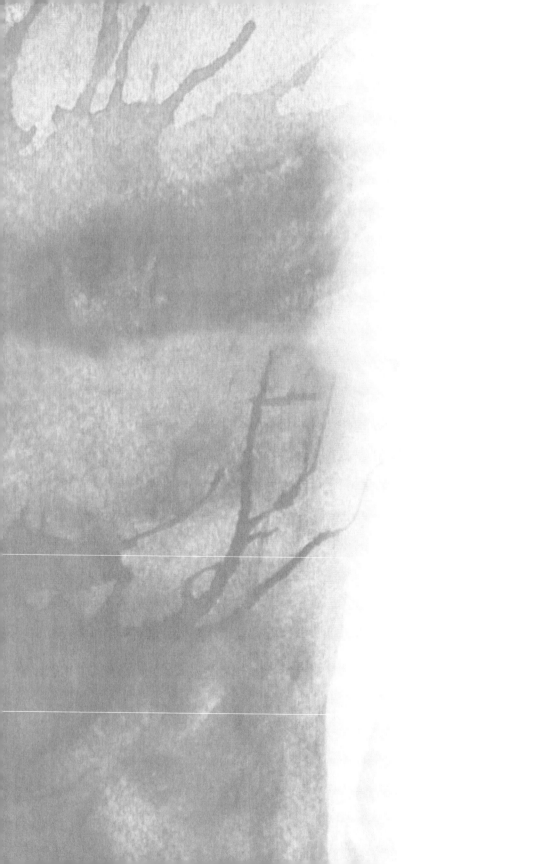

CHAPTER 1

Transforming the Approach

*"And lead us not into
temptation, but deliver us
from evil."* – MATTHEW 6:13A

With these words millions around the world pray each day for the grace and strength to see and avoid temptation and to be delivered from the actions of those people and situations that intend to do us harm. Even those who do not use these words sometimes call for the intervention of a higher power in their lives in a way that fulfills the request that is in this prayer. One of the greatest risks, one of the most devastating evils that we and our children face is an evil in our midst. It is a threat to our children from inside the places and spaces that are supposed to protect and care for them. In the shadows of those environments are those who threaten to molest our children. Surely the words of this powerful prayer echo our hope for our children and the children around us.

The purpose of the book is to provide adults with information about the ways they can prevent child sexual abuse by recognizing and putting a stop to that evil. Up until now, adults have concentrated their efforts on learning how to recognize when a child has already been molested, how to deal with disclosures, and how to report suspected abuse. Now we want to turn our attention to the adults who interact with our children so we can learn to recognize them before abuse occurs and prevent harm to our children.

Child molesters, living among us in our homes, our neighborhoods, and our communities, tempt our children and pull them into circumstances and situations that occur for them as hopeless traps with no way out. These same adults tempt us into believing and trusting them and, in many cases, into willingly handing over to them the most precious and vulnerable among us—our children. They tempt us with their charismatic ways, their ability to make us believe they are genuinely concerned about children, their compassion for our situation, and their skill in manipulating those around them, including us, to see them as loving, concerned adults who just want to help out.

These chameleons hide in plain sight behind their "normal" appearance. They use their ability to weave their way into our lives and the lives of our children to prey upon our children. When they act, the consequences are devastating, and the scars remain for a lifetime.

My compelling interest

People often ask me why I am so passionate about this issue. They want to know why I would spend over 40 years of my life looking for ways to create and nurture safe environments for children at risk. The next question is usually, "Are you a survivor?" For many, the most logical explanation is that I am a survivor. However, I was never molested and neither was anyone in my immediate family. My passion comes from my relationship with a young female runaway I met in Southeastern Oklahoma in the early 1970's.

As part of an effort to create a place for abused, neglected, runaway, or homeless youth other than the adult jails they were being held in at the time, I volunteered on a team creating a community based shelter in my county. The purpose of the program was to provide an alternative for young people and children, and to create an alternative that kept young runaways and troubled youth out of adult jails.

I assumed the responsibility of Volunteer Coordinator and in that capacity, a local Juvenile Court Judge asked me to step in and provide advocacy and support for a young woman he had concerns about. The girl, whom we will call Carla, was a runaway, and had been determined through court proceedings to be a "Child in Need of Supervision." However, the reason she ran away was that her home life was intolerable and she did not know what else to do.

At that time there were no programs like Court Appointed Special Advocates (CASA) to provide that service for the child and the court. This forward thinking Judge knew this young woman had potential but he also faced a dilemma that was plaguing juvenile courts at the time. There were really not many options available for a young person in Carla's situation. The Judge decided to try something new and asked me to take on the job and see whether it could make a difference for Carla. I was willing to step out into unfamiliar territory and reach out to her for the same reason.

My husband and young children openly welcomed her into our lives. For them, she was just someone new we got to have fun with and spend time with. The children never knew why she came to visit us or what her own home was like and she got to be a normal kid, doing normal things for a few hours a week.

Through the months that she was part of our lives, I saw firsthand the suffering of a child living in degrading and often depraved circumstances. Although her father did not abuse her, he was a sexual pervert and a drunk. She was a well-developed 13-year-old whose body suggested she was closer to 18 years old. Her father encouraged other men in his life to notice her. She had no female role model—except me, for the time I was in her life—and no connection with a normal family except the time she spent with us. She was the target of seduction efforts from her father's friends and acquaintances, and she spent a lot of her time finding ways to fend off their advances and protect herself from being assaulted. Her efforts were valiant but not always successful.

Eventually, she was removed to foster care and I was no longer in contact with her. However, the experience of listening to her speak matter-of-factly about things she should not even have known about, and realizing that she had no one in her home or her family that would protect her, was the catalyst for my commitment to this effort. It was Carla who triggered my compelling interest in finding a way to make sure that children never have to fear sexual assault from people whom they should be able to trust.

Although I do not know what happened to Carla or how her life turned out, I can never forget the haunted look in her eyes and the deadness in her voice when we first met. I can also see, in my mind's eye, the laughter and joy in her face when we took her with us on a trip to the park with our children or invited her to have a simple dinner with us at home around a dining room table. Those brief moments of joy and life in her otherwise hopeless existence became the seeds for my compelling interest in this issue.

As a result, I have been pursuing a vision ever since- a vision of a world where no child has to fear being sexually assaulted by someone responsible for taking care of them. Preventing child sexual abuse begins with understanding the nature and scope of the problem. Just as with any prevention effort, we must begin with a thorough understanding of the problem. Knowing what we are dealing with is essential to the creation of an effective plan for prevention.

The nature of the problem

This is not a new inquiry. Since the late 1970s and early 1980s, professionals in the field of child sexual abuse prevention and investigation have been looking for effective ways to prevent this kind of abuse and treat the fallout of this abuse for victims. In 1984, Dr. David Finkelhor laid the groundwork for this work in his book *Child Sexual Abuse: New Theory and Research*. In his book, Dr. Finkelhor identified four essential elements that must be present before child sexual abuse can happen:

1. A potential molester must have some motivation to sexually abuse a child.

2. The potential molester must overcome any internal inclination to hold back or stop before acting on that desire or motivation.

3. The potential molester must overcome any external or environmental obstacles to committing sexual abuse.

4. The potential molester or some other thing must undermine or overcome any resistance the child exhibits.

There is virtually nothing that adults can do to eliminate the first two of these four elements from the picture. We have no control over someone else's desires or needs.

In addition, although we can educate everyone about the nature and scope of this problem and encourage those who have these sexual desires to get help, we can't force anyone to take actions to keep themselves from acting on their desire for sexual or romantic contact with a child. Individuals experiencing those thoughts and feelings must take personal responsibility for dealing with these two elements.

Nevertheless, there is hope for the future. For example, research shows that once a juvenile sex offender is identified and provided with appropriate intervention, the rate of recidivism is very, very low. In one major study, only 9.7% of juvenile offenders were subsequently arrested for sexual assault as an adult. Someday, if we pay close attention and take action when we have concerns about young people, it may be possible to intervene early enough with juveniles to stop the development of an adult child molester.

However, if we are to prevent child sexual abuse now, we need to concentrate on the elements that we *can* impact. Because all four are necessary for child sexual abuse to occur, eliminating two of the elements could put a stop to most child sexual abuse.

As adults, we can set up roadblocks and obstacles for child molesters in our environments. We can create an environment where there is no opportunity for child sexual abuse to occur. We can learn to recognize the behaviors that indicate someone is a risk of harm to children and young people, and interrupt potentially risky situations. We can establish and enforce policies and procedures that promote openness and encourage group participation. We can encourage others to drop in on us on those rare occasions when we are meeting alone with other peoples' children. We can create and insist on compliance with codes of conduct that establishes boundaries and guidelines for our interactions with children in our environment. We can carefully screen all adults who have access to our children, and we can be willing to speak up when something just doesn't feel right.

In addition to establishing barriers and obstacles that interrupt the efforts of child molesters to get access to children, we can talk with our children about these dangers. We can teach them the "touching rules" and let them know that these are important personal safety rules just like the rules for fire safety and bicycle safety and protecting ourselves in other areas of life. We can continue to make sure that our schools, religious education programs, and youth service organizations such as Boy Scouts, Camp Fire, and Big Brother/Big Sister programs are providing children with information that reinforces important personal safety messages.

If we put our efforts into creating environments where there is no opportunity for a molester to gain access to a child, we can interrupt the cycle of abuse. We can teach our children to say "no" or words that mean "no" to any touch or situation that is confusing, or makes them feel uncomfortable. We can teach our children that they can leave the situation when it gets uncomfortable, and we can train them to tell a trusted adult when someone makes them feel uncomfortable, confuses them, or hurts them for no good reason. When children learn these rules, it will be more difficult for a child molester to prey on them.

For the past 15 to 20 years, the emphasis has been on teaching children to resist the overtures of a child molester. It is time that adults take on the primary responsibility for preventing child sexual abuse and protecting children from sexual predators.

In order to accomplish this goal, we must be willing to become adept at learning to recognize people who are a risk of harm to children and young people, and at interrupting the flow of their "grooming process." We must keep our eyes on our surroundings and notice both the physical environment and the actions of other adults who interact with the children in our homes, our neighborhoods, our schools, and our communities.

Becoming adept or proficient in this area requires that we be willing to take the actions necessary to develop and perfect our skills and abilities. This means that we must apply the tools of *Developing 20/20 Foresight*© to the problem by:

1. Identifying a compelling interest or passion for becoming an expert in this area.

2. Gathering information that will help us identify and stop molesters.

3. Practicing the tools we learn about.

4. Paying attention to what's happening in our environment.

5. Being flexible in dealing with challenging people and situations.

If we apply these tools to the problem, we will hone our ability to recognize people and situations that put children at risk of sexual assault, and we can begin

6. Operating "in the zone" in our efforts to protect children from abuse.

Through this book, we will apply these steps in developing proficiency to the problem of stopping predators from abusing our children and the children of our communities.

CHAPTER 2

Discover a Compelling Interest

Whose job is it?

Obviously, no one wants children to be sexually abused, but why should you spend your time concentrating on this issue? After all, you are a responsible adult. You take excellent care of the children in your life. You would never leave them alone with a shady character or entrust them to someone who would do them harm.

You watch over them. You meet their friends and the other adults in their life. You make sure that events are well chaperoned. You don't put your children in harm's way and you genuinely care about other people's children. You make sure that the people who work or volunteer with you at work or on projects are responsible people who would never harm a child. So, why should you invest time in becoming proficient in this area?

There are two short answers to that question.

The first is: every child and every family is vulnerable to the grooming process of a child molester.

The second is: child sexual abuse is a societal issue that must be tackled by all of us as a public health issue if we are to stop it from happening to our children.

Though the answers are simple, the pathway to becoming proficient in dealing with them is more complex. Let's look at these *simple* answers and begin to get an idea about what it will take to stop predators from sexually abusing our children.

Every child is vulnerable

Research tells us that one out of every five girls and one out of every ten boys will be molested by the time they are 18 years old. (St. Vincent's Hospital 2001; Finkelhor, 1994) In addition, it is very likely that the person who molests them will be someone they are biologically related to or they know and trust. According to studies, 29 percent of child sexual abuse is incest, meaning the perpetrator and the victim are related by blood. Another 60 percent of child sexual abuse is committed by people who are known and trusted by both the children and their parents or guardians. Only 11 percent of the sexual assaults on our children are committed by strangers. (Russell, 2000)

One reason this is sometimes difficult for us to appreciate is that so much media attention is paid to stranger abductions. A child is snatched off the street by an unknown assailant or lured to a secret meeting by someone they meet online. This is news because the events are dramatic and unusual and the outcome is rarely good.

The problem is that this media focus on stranger abductions and Internet predators begins to shape how the community thinks about the problem of child sexual abuse. The thousands of reports of sexual abuse that are being handled every day by child protection officials, police officers, and families often find their way into the news only as part of the research basis for an in-depth investigative story or because a child was seriously injured or killed by an abuser.

That is the nature of "news." Stranger abductions are newsworthy events and so is the ability of predators to connect with children through the Internet. (Wolak, Mitchell, & Finkelhor, 2006) When a child is abducted or drawn into a dangerous meeting with an Internet predator, law enforcement seeks out media attention as part of the concentrated effort to find the child and to teach parents about the dangers of unsupervised Internet activity for their children. This media attention is often the only chance the child has for survival in the situation.

When these events are the primary source of our information about child sexual abuse, many can and often do conclude that most sexual assaults on children are committed by strangers who snatch them off streets or out of playgrounds. From that frame of reference or in that context, we start to believe if we simply pay attention, we can prevent those things from happening.

Sexual predators that stalk and abduct our children from playgrounds, neighborhoods, and shopping malls are obviously very dangerous. Children often do not survive those abductions. In the same way, Internet predators are becoming more and more creative every day. They continue to improve other methods of reaching into our homes and plucking children from our midst. We need to learn all we can about how to prevent these crimes and protect our children from these situations.

However, focusing our attention on these two risks leaves us with a big problem. More than 85 percent of the sexual assaults on our children do not involve strangers or abductions or the Internet. (Russell & Bolen, 2000) These assaults are the result of the carefully orchestrated actions of someone who grooms either children they are related to by blood or children they know well.

Once we come face to face with the real nature of the risk and a view of the true danger to our children, we are confronted with what can only be described as a compelling interest in preventing this abuse. The place to start to accomplish this goal is to deal with all the myths and preconceived notions we already have about sexual predators. We must confront what we think we know about those who molest children and gather information that can help us recognize the potential predators in our midst.

Unfortunately, no one can tell simply by looking that someone is a child molester. There are no tell-tale signs.

Child molesters are not disheveled, crazy men, with wild eyes. They are the people next door, the coach or teacher everyone loves, aunts and uncles who are always there for us. They are male, female, rich, poor, married, single, and they come in all sizes, shapes, and cultures.

They exploit our needs and prey on the vulnerabilities of our children. They convince us they love the children and would do anything for them. They convince our children that the children are to blame for anything "bad" that happens so children who are molested live in a cloud of shame for most of their lives.

Child molesters usually are talented, gifted people who have a great way of getting kids to trust them. In fact, they use the same methods used by those with a completely pure motive to their actions. A child molester may spend the first meeting with a child just getting to know about the child's interests and may be heard encouraging a child to do well in some endeavor. This person will be careful to speak to the child as a child. For example, the child molester will talk with first graders at a first grade level just like those of us who are genuinely interested in the well-being of children.

In the beginning, a potential child molester may look no different from any of us. This person appears caring and generous and takes time to develop relationships with the child and with the parents, guardians, or other responsible parties. Parents and other adults often come to rely on this person as someone who really cares about children. The molester uses that leverage with parents to further pull the child, the family, and the community into their web of deceit through the "grooming" process.

Although, as you will see later in the book, there are behaviors that are common to child molesters, they each have their own version of the grooming process. Regardless of the way they go about it, molesters each have their own pattern of gaining control over children and families. The goal is always the same; convince the child, the family, and the community that the molester is someone who can be trusted to be alone with children.

We have seen that many of the tools responsible adults use for initiating relationships with children also are used by child molesters. There is nothing wrong with these tools; they are the most effective ways to establish connections with the children we want to work with or support. What we need to be aware of is that for a molester, these tools are the first step in a much larger process of grooming children, parents, and the community. That is why it is so difficult to identify potential molesters in the initial stages of their grooming process. They look just like the rest of us at first.

However, the molester is not satisfied with establishing a good healthy relationship. Child predators use that part of the process to kick off a much bigger game. In fact, some have described this first encounter as the "initial contact." This phrase gives us some insight into the methodical planning and manipulation that makes up the grooming process.

Others who use the phrase "initial contact" include undercover police officers, con artists, promoters, scammers, etc. The common thread for all these is that they have a hidden agenda. They are out to accomplish an objective that is deliberately hidden from the potential target's view. This is exactly how child molesters work, and why it is so difficult to identify their real motives.

The grooming process for a molester includes three separate elements that all happen at the same time.

Physical grooming: Through the grooming process, predators gradually break down a child's resistance to touch. The initial contact may be simply a pat on the back or a handshake — anything that gets the predator's hands on the child. However, the touching does not stop there. Over time, the touching becomes more and more intimate, until the child is pressed into a relationship that involves intimate sexual touching.

The reason this process works is that it is not just about the touching. If the only aspect of the grooming process involved touching, most children would run away from anyone who got too "friendly" with them. However, while the touching is progressing, the molester is engaged in the second piece of the grooming process: the psychological grooming. The psychological grooming breaks down the child's resistance to intimate touches.

Psychological Grooming: Psychological grooming often begins with the initial contact with the child in what seems like, and usually is, a harmless way. An introduction at a school, church, or community event can start the process, or perhaps the child molester has volunteered to coach, teach, tutor, or mentor a child. As long as the intent of the relationship is healthy and wholesome, these activities represent the best of society. The problem is it is hard to know the adult's intentions from the beginning. For that reason, we must learn how to recognize the behavioral warning signs of potentially risky adults and maintain a healthy suspicion of all adults who interact with our children and the children around us.

In addition to the normal, predictable ways of creating relatedness with children, there is one way that a child molester can drive a wedge between a child and a parent, guardian, or other caregiver quickly and with relative ease. Child molesters know it is easy to get into a child's life by simply agreeing with the child when he or she is upset with parents or other authority figures.

Every day parents, guardians, and other caregivers deal with children being upset because someone said "no." Parents, guardians, and other caregivers make decisions about what children want and what they can have based on lots of different factors. Children only know they want what they want when they want it, and they get upset when the parent or caregiver says "no," "maybe," or "we'll see."

A child molester sees this situation as an opening for quickly gaining influence over the child. All that is necessary is for the molester to agree with the child and not the adults. The child now has the agreement of an adult, who is trusted by the other adults in the environment, and who disagrees with the parent, guardian, or caregiver. The molester instantly has broken down any of the child's natural barriers or resistance to trusting an adult the child does not know really well — and the parent has no idea this has happened.

Regardless of how the molester initiates the relationship with the child, the psychological grooming is just getting started. Molesters use various psychological tools to convince children they love them and only have their best interests at heart. They tell the children their actions are motivated by love. They indulge the children by giving them gifts and letting them do things their parents will not allow. Once they drive the wedge between parent and child, they do whatever it takes to continue to widen the gap and insert themselves between the child and the parent.

In addition to using psychological tools to convince children they are truly loved by the molester, molesters also use psychological grooming to:

- Convince children they are to blame for what is happening.

- Convince children that no one will believe them if they tell. After all, it will be their word against that of a respected adult.

- Convince children they will get in trouble if they tell anyone what is happening.

- Convince children that telling will result in the child or the adult being taken away, and will upset the family or the community.

If, at any point in the process, the child threatens to tell, the molester may bully the child into silence by threatening to do harm to something or someone the child loves. The child may believe that a parent, friend, sibling, or even a well-loved pet is at risk of harm from the molester if the child speaks up.

All these psychological games are going on at the same time the molester is becoming more and more aggressive and intimate with touching the child. In addition, the molester never takes his or her eye off the adults in the community. In fact, a key piece of the grooming process is the community grooming.

Community Grooming: This third element of the process is going on simultaneously with the physical and psychological grooming. While the molester is gradually becoming more intimate with physical contact with the child, and trapping the child in the cycle of abuse using psychological tools, the community and parents are being subjected to a talented display of manipulation and control.

The molester uses tools such as helping with homework, offering to drive the kids to soccer practice, or offering to take the children for a Saturday afternoon to give the parents or guardians some time to themselves. A study of teachers who molest found that those who commit this crime usually also had awards on their walls for being an "outstanding teacher" or the "most popular teacher." They were the ones everyone loved — the ones who couldn't possibly be guilty of this kind of crime.

There are many, many ways a molester can curry favor with the adults in a child's life and divert attention from the molester's real objectives. As this community grooming progresses, the child sees what is happening and is further convinced that the molester is right — no one would believe the child if he or she spoke up. In the child's eyes, telling would make no difference, and when the child is convinced of that, the molester has won the game. The child is now trapped in the cycle of abuse and the molester moves on to the next step.

When we carefully examine the thorough and effective job a child molester does to lay the groundwork for molesting a child without being caught, we realize that all children are at risk. The actions of a child molester are not the acts of irrational criminals. They are well thought-out, methodical, and manipulative. The child molester's interest is in a particular child, with particular characteristics, and a perceived vulnerability. Once those characteristics are identified, the child molester goes to work to accomplish the goal.

Realizing that these are cunning and effective people who are masters of manipulation is often a jolt because now even our children — the ones we have worked so hard to protect — are at risk. Protecting the children in our environments from sexual abuse is more than a good idea; it is our individual and collective responsibility, and we have a compelling interest in becoming proficient at recognizing risky adults.

It's a public health issue

If we limit our view of the problem of child sexual abuse to what we can do as individuals, we can't really expect to stop it everywhere. But seeing beyond our own children and the need to keep them safe sometimes is difficult. Besides, what we are talking about here is sexual abuse, and a child sexual abuse epidemic is not the same as a smallpox epidemic — or is it?

Unfortunately, or fortunately as the case may be, the two things are both different and the same. They are different because one deals with a disease that is serious, contagious, and most often fatal. The other, child sexual abuse, is a behavior that causes serious problems but is neither contagious nor usually fatal for the perpetrators or the victims.

However, the only way to stop both smallpox and child sexual abuse is prevention. Vaccinating against smallpox was the only way to *prevent* that disease — and it worked. There is no explicit treatment for smallpox, but the prevention efforts have virtually eliminated the disease from society today. The last case of smallpox in the United States was in 1949, and a 1977 case in Somalia was the last known case in the world. In fact, medical professionals no longer vaccinate for smallpox because it has been prevented. The only way for smallpox to come back is for someone to deliberately introduce it back into society. Prevention has succeeded in eradicating smallpox from the world.

Prevention also is the only way to stop child sexual abuse. Educating adults about how to recognize risky adult behaviors, establishing and enforcing guidelines for creating safe environments, and teaching children to resist the overtures of a predator are the ways we can *prevent* child sexual abuse. Anything else leaves us dealing with the consequences of abuse after the fact. But for almost 30 years child sexual abuse prevention efforts have been focused on teaching children to say "no," run away, and tell a trusted adult about what happened. Adult education efforts have centered on teaching adults how to recognize children who might have already been abused, how to deal with disclosures, and how to report suspected abuse.

Don't get the wrong idea here. *It is very important for adults to know how and when to report suspected abuse, how to respond to disclosures of abuse from a child, and how to recognize the behavioral and physical signs that a child has been molested.* There will be information about that in a later chapter. However, knowing those things will not stop abuse before it happens and stopping it before the child has to suffer the consequences should be our objective.

If we only learn how to respond when a child tells us about being abused, or we only educate ourselves about how to report suspected abuse, we will not prevent child sexual abuse from occurring. In the same way, learning what to do if someone exhibits the symptoms of smallpox or knowing how to report suspected cases will not prevent smallpox. The only thing that stops something before it happens is "prevention."

If we continue to deal with this issue in a personal or individual way, it will have an impact in our own lives but it will not stop child sexual abuse from happening in the world. The only way to have any chance of putting a stop to this kind of assault is to bring it out into the public eye and begin to relate to it as a public health issue or a societal problem.

In a later chapter, we will discuss some of the obstacles to dealing with child sexual abuse as a public health issue. For now, we want to look at how we go about bringing the issue of child sexual abuse prevention into the public conversation as an issue of concern for all of society.

The Centers for Disease Control and Prevention says that analyzing an issue from a public health perspective requires a systematic approach that has four steps:

1. Define the problem

2. Identify risk and protective factors

3. Develop and test prevention strategies

4. Assure widespread adoption of prevention principles and strategies.

We could take the time and methodically analyze the nature of the problem until we all agreed that this is definitely a public health issue. In the alternative, we could just look at the facts about child sexual abuse and agree that this issue meets the criteria.

The problem is that there are adults in our communities who either prefer to have sexual or romantic relationships with children or who don't stop themselves from acting on their inappropriate emotional and sexual attractions to children in times of crisis or stress. The problem impacts a substantial part of our population.

As we saw earlier, one out of five females and one out of ten males are likely to be sexually molested before they are 18 years old. Using these figures, which some consider conservative, we can estimate that there are 40 million adult survivors of child sexual abuse in the United States alone. (Finkelhor, 1993) According to the US Census Bureau, total population estimates for the United States as of October 17, 2006, are that approximately 296 million people live in this country. An estimated 25 percent of those people are under the age of 18. (U.S. Census Bureau) So, that means 13.5 percent of the adult population is suffering from the effects of this trauma and an estimated 2.5 million children who will be molested before they turn 18. If we were talking about any other health issue affecting such a large segment of the population, it unquestionably would be considered a public health issue and would be the subject of widespread efforts to intervene and interrupt the pattern.

However, there are a couple of pieces of the puzzle that do not seem to fit easily into the typical "public health issue" paradigm. One sticky piece is the fact that it sometimes is difficult for the public to consider any kind violence to be a "public health issue." People prefer to view violence from a criminal perspective only.

The CDC does not see it that way. They see injury and violence as preventable. They apply the same concepts to injury and violence prevention as they utilize to address the threat of infectious disease. According to the CDC, injuries and violence are preventable, and the same scientific methods apply to dealing with these issues as are used to deal with any other preventable health issue.

The problem is that the threat of harm for more than 85 percent of the victims is not from bacteria or poor sanitation. The threat is from people, and the people who are a threat are people we know and trust — a member of the family, a trusted coach or teacher, a minister, a friend, or a neighbor.

In addition, the assault is sexual, and society seems to react differently to sexual assaults. People often blame the victim. They say things like, "I can't believe that happened," or "She brought it on herself with the way she dresses."

Even perpetrators blame the victims, and we all know that defense attorneys put victims on trial to justify sexual assaults. The community speculates about why the child or young person did not tell someone or stop the perpetrator from the beginning, or they wonder why the perpetrator's spouse did not stop the abuse. All of these reactions conspire to turn attention from the real culprit — the child molester — and they conspire to mask the true nature of the offense as a crime against society and a public health issue.

Dealing with child sexual abuse as a public health issue accomplishes several valuable objectives. First, it takes the "taint" off the sexual nature of the assault and puts the attention where it should be, on the perpetrator. Second, it allows us to talk about the subject openly and explore ways to prevent these incidents from occurring. Third, it refocuses our primary efforts on preventing the abuse. Fourth, it increases our chances of making a difference with this issue by having our attention on having adults learn how to prevent sexual abuse.

Having effective systems for prosecuting and punishing those who molest children is critical, and creating successful treatment options for victims and offenders is a key piece of a comprehensive program to deal with this issue. However, neither of these approaches will ever prevent sexual abuse from happening.

In order to prevent child sexual abuse, we must deal with it as a public health issue, and one purpose of this book and the programs it promotes is to do just that by identifying the risk factors, identifying new prevention strategies, and creating ways of implementing these strategies throughout the adult community.

We begin by identifying risky adult behaviors and outlining steps to take when someone exhibits those behaviors. When the risky adult behaviors are identified, and people know how to react and respond to any adult who exhibits those behaviors, we are on the path to preventing child sexual abuse.

The job of creating a safe environment for our children is an important challenge. Protecting our children is not just *our* job; it's everybody's job. It is in the best interests of our children and our society that we identify or create a compelling interest in becoming proficient in our ability to identify risky adult behaviors and intervene to prevent abuse. As caring adults, it is up to us to identify that interest and act consistent with a desire to make a difference.

In Chapter 1, I shared with you how I developed a compelling interest in this issue. Where will you look to find your compelling interest? Will you find it in the bright eyes and loving embrace of your own child? Will the well being and commitment to your children having the opportunity to grow up without this threat in their lives be enough, or will it take more?

Perhaps the plight of a friend whose child is victimized will help you see the need for all of us to become experts in this area. Perhaps you will see a story on television that compels you to take action. For some, the realization that the problem of child sexual abuse is a public health issue that has been neglected by adults for far too long will trigger the need to learn all you can and become part of the solution.

No matter how the compelling interest is created, that you develop one is key to becoming proficient in recognizing adults who are a risk of harm to children and learning how to intervene before the abuse occurs. Once we are clear that this issue warrants our focus and attention, we must begin to learn about the behaviors to watch for in adults around us and develop strategies for intervening when risky situations arise.

CHAPTER 3

Evil Speaks for Itself

If we are to develop expertise and become proficient in our ability to recognize people who are a possible risk of harm to children and intervene before abuse occurs, we need to go to the source. This does not mean we need to go interview child molesters ourselves. Several research articles and books have been written about child molesters that can help us identify the particular characteristics and warning signs that require our attention.

In 1984, Dr. David Finkelhor, noted child sexual abuse expert, in discussing what was known about the characteristics of child molesters at that time pointed out that many of our perceptions or old ideas about child molesters may need to be re-examined and revised. He noted:

> *"We are particularly uncomfortable with the fact that so much of what we know about sexual abusers comes from men in prison and in treatment. When information is gathered about undetected molesters, the picture may change drastically."*

Perhaps one of the main reasons the characteristics of child molesters are so hard to identify is that molesters lead double lives. In the community, they often are responsible, model citizens. They cultivate relationships with parents, families, and other responsible adults in order to diffuse any possible concern that might arise about their behavior.

In fact, one offender said that he pays particular attention to the parents and others in the community when he is molesting a child. If there is any indication that someone is getting concerned or even suspicious of his interactions with or friendship with the child, he immediately modifies his behavior to eliminate the concern. He will put some distance between himself and child — at least in front of others. He will spend less time with the child alone for awhile. He will stop putting his arm around the child or hugging the child in public for a time until he can see that parents or other adults are at ease with him again. After that, it is business as usual again. Parents trust him again and children, seeing this, are convinced that they will not be believed if they speak up — so they keep quiet.

Deception is the key for most child molesters. In fact, Salter, in his 2003 book, *Predators: Pedophiles, Rapists, and other Sex Offenders — Who they are, how they operate, and how we can protect ourselves and our children*, concluded from his interviews and research, "If it is in the offender's best interests to lie, and if he can do it and not get caught, he will lie."

As we said earlier, our best bet for finding effective ways to prevent child sexual abuse is to thoroughly know and understand the nature of the problem. Unfortunately, that means talking with child molesters and finding out how they accomplish their goal of molesting a child. These interviews are our best chance of finding ways to teach adults how to prevent child sexual abuse. Offenders can tell us a lot about prevention by telling us about how they do what they do and what they rely on to gain access to children.

One of the first efforts to discover what child molesters have to say about molesting children is found in the results of a research study from 1989. (Conte, Wolfe, Smith, 1989) In interviews with a small group of men participating in a community-based specialized sex offender treatment program, researchers searched for information about the following areas:

- Selecting victims
- Process for engaging children in abuse
- Measures used to maintain the victim's participation and secrecy

Through these interviews, child molesters admitted:

- They rarely molested a stranger. The victims were children they were related to or knew well.
- The factors that entered into their choice of victims included certain preferred physical characteristics, the child's level of vulnerability and friendliness, and the willingness to trust.
- When options were available, they chose either the youngest child or the one that appeared needy.
- They selected victims who were not likely to tell.
- They convinced themselves that what they were doing was okay.
- The engaged in play, talk, and touch to get comfortable with the child.
- They used off-color jokes and language and showed pornography to trap and silence the child.
- When all else failed, they threatened harm to the child, or something or someone the child loved.
- They isolated children to enhance control.
  (Conte, et al.)

When asked what they would include in a manual on how to molest a child, these child molesters added a number of activities that are intended to befriend and seduce children. They suggested having a wide repertoire of conversations to use with children, from sympathy to talking about sex. One important thread through all the ideas was looking for apparent deficiencies in the child's relationship with parents or with the child's home life. (Conte, et al.)

The child molesters also talked about the need to infiltrate the family and "make nice with" the parents. They looked at situations that could be exploited such as a family in which children are not really heard or were isolated or ignored. The molesters suggested those situations were opportunities to drive a wedge between children and parents and to develop powerful bonds with children. (Conte, et al.)

This early study was the beginning of our efforts to learn what child molesters have to say about how they choose and groom their victims. Child molesters have been telling us how they do what they do for a long time through their words and actions. However, this was a circumstance that demonstrated the old adage that "knowing makes no difference." We had no way to transmit that information to adults in the community in a way that was useful and effective.

In addition, between 2000 and 2002, the National Catholic Risk Retention Group, Inc. funded research on this issue as part of a project to develop an adult child sexual abuse prevention program for the Roman Catholic Church in the United States. Part of that research included a root cause analysis of approximately 500 cases of child molestation and interviews with almost 100 child molesters. One of the primary objectives of this process was to determine whether there were typical behaviors exhibited by child molesters that could be identified and interrupted.

When you need the best information, it is always a good idea to go to the source. In this case, the source is a group of people who admit to lying when it is in their best interests, and whose purpose is to seduce our children for their own sexual gratification. If we are committed to dealing with this issue in a way that prevents future harm to children, we must take the information child molesters provide and create a pathway for our own education and training. Child sexual abuse is a serious problem for all children in society, and stopping molesters is a monumental task that we can achieve only by working together to find answers to very difficult problems.

In this effort, our two greatest assets are the child molesters who share with us their tools and techniques, and our knowledge of how adults learn. Making the best use of both of these resources provides that pathway we are seeking. Finding an effective way to accomplish our mission is the greatest challenge.

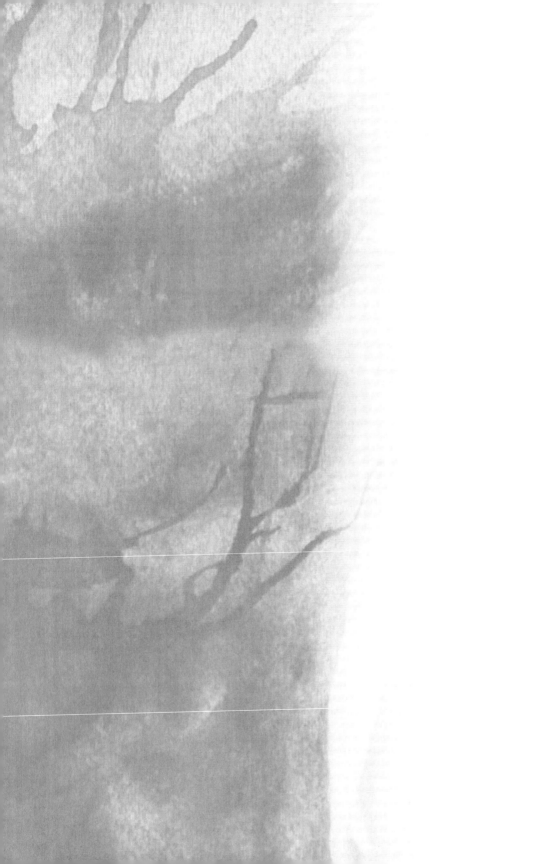

CHAPTER 4

Identifying Potential Predators

Recognizing that child sexual abuse is a problem that needs our attention and there are no easy answers is just the beginning. When we realize it is up to us to protect children, it becomes clear that we don't know how to accomplish this goal. We don't know who and what the risk is to our children, and we don't know which adults present a problem and which do not. Many of us grew up learning about "stranger danger" and some of us learned the touching rules. However, learning, as adults, how to recognize the potentially risky behavior of adults in our environments is a brand new endeavor.

Confronting the scope of this problem can be overwhelming. However, applying the tools of *Developing 20/20 Foresight* to this issue means that we use all our resources to gather information and to learn all we can about the people who threaten the well-being of our children.

Clearly, identifying the characteristics of a potential predator is the first step in the process of gathering the information needed to become someone who can prevent child sexual abuse. Some may think that is the easy part, a conclusion based on false perceptions such as these:

- Shouldn't we be able to recognize most potential child molesters by the way they look? Everyone knows child molesters are "crazy." These people are definitely not in their right mind and it is easy to see when someone is just not right. Child molesters don't look normal, do they? And even those few who *look* normal are recognizable because they are not like us. People like us don't do this kind of thing to children.

- If you can't tell some of them are a problem just by the way they look you should be able to tell them from normal people anyway, right? Surely they are from a lower socio-economic group. They aren't really like us. They must be uneducated or even illiterate. Rational, educated people would never do this to children.

- How about the homosexual community? Shouldn't we be concerned about this group? After all, aren't they more likely to molest children than someone like us?

- What about the parents of victims? If they just did a better job, or mothers stayed home to take care of children, or parents were better at supervising their children's activities on the Internet, children would be safe from this type of assault, right?

All of these myths and preconceived notions get in the way of us gathering the information we need to identify potentially risky adults and learn how to intervene when adults exhibit these behaviors. Adults often are inclined to substitute their opinions or points of view for facts and research. In this case, operating as if our opinions and points of view are "facts" about child molesters increases the risk to our children.

For example, regardless of substantial evidence to the contrary, some people go to great lengths to try and blame the homosexual community for the problem of child sexual abuse. Although a number of studies address this issue, the simplest fact that dispels this notion is that most abusers are male and most victims are female. (Conte, et al.) (Russell, et al.)

This does not mean homosexuals do not molest children; it just means that identifying a suspect group is not a productive way to identify a potentially risky adult. When we blame a "group" for this crime, we focus our attention on that group, and all the others who are exhibiting risky behaviors have free reign to go forward. We aren't paying any attention to them.

Most of us still believe some or all of these notions about which adults pose a risk of harm to our children. We are very quick to point a finger at someone or something as *the* reason when things go wrong or when a child is molested. Perhaps we attach a label to an individual, a group, or a situation in order to demonstrate how *we* are different, *we* are *right*, and *we* are not like those others. Or perhaps we just need to believe that these predators could not be people we know and trust. If they are, we would have to admit that our children are more vulnerable than we thought possible and we don't really know how to protect them. However, admitting this is key to our commitment to preventing child sexual abuse.

How we relate to this issue is no different than how we relate to many other things that challenge or confront us in our lives. We seem to need to rush to find *the* answer to all kinds of questions. All around us, people are quick to judge and assess what's wrong, and even quicker to attribute problems to some specific cause. Perhaps we should consider whether the need to rush to judgment is a symbol of our impatience or an indication of our anxiety. We are anxious about things we don't know for certain. We are anxious about things that are out of our control. We are anxious about the uncertainty of life and the uncertainty in our environments. And, we want answers, NOW!

However, although impatience contributes to this rush to judgment, it is much more likely that fear and anxiety cause us to find something or someone to blame for the problems of the world. The problem is that each time we decide some specific thing is *the* cause, we end up with a new, often bigger problem.

Child sexual abuse is not an exception to this rule. When we blame child sexual abuse on bad parenting, homosexuality, or any other neatly-defined reason, group, or thing, we play into the hands of child molesters because most offenders do not fit neatly into any particular category. When we limit our view only to those groups we think of as potentially risky adults, we take our eyes off the things that really can make the difference in our commitment to prevent child sexual abuse.

Most child molesters are socially gifted people who have a genuine rapport with children and well-developed skills in relating to children, and grooming the adults in the community. They ingratiate themselves into the lives of the children and their families as part of their seduction of the children.

The problem is that when we start to realize anyone could be a child molester, we begin to see threats to our children everywhere. It is important to remember that not everyone is a risk to children. Caring about children does not mean someone is a threat to children. In fact, it is important to identify those that really care about kids and encourage them.

Being interested in children also doesn't automatically mean someone is a child molester. If we look carefully at the people who have molested children, the only characteristic that they have in common is that they molest children. The things about them that indicate they are a possible risk to kids are evident in their behavior.

As a result, none of the typical characteristics, such as ethnic group, sexual preference, or educational background, will help us identify the risky adults in our homes, schools, and communities. This does not mean there is no way to recognize potentially risky adults. It just means the identifiers we think are relevant are not the ones we should be paying attention to! It also reinforces the need for all adults to maintain a "healthy" suspicion about other adults in the environment who interact with children and youth.

What does it mean to "maintain a healthy suspicion?" One analogy that might give some insight here is to think about what happens when you are driving. In the beginning, when we learned to drive, we were ultra-conscientious about everything. Remember how anxious you were simply driving down a two-lane road? After all, it seemed like everyone was coming right at you and would hit you head-on any minute.

Then you got on the freeway, and all of a sudden there was a new anxiety. The cars on both sides of you were closing in. Surely you would get squeezed between them and that would be the end of that.

However, over time, you learned to recognize what might be called the "parameters of normal" for others on the highway. You learned to recognize the drivers who were behaving erratically, those who simply were not paying attention, and those who were no risk at all. So, your time behind the wheel became much more enjoyable. You were not anxious all the time — but you were alert to possible problems and if someone was driving in a way that was outside those boundaries of normal, you automatically reverted to the defensive driving techniques and tools learned long ago. As a result, you avoid most accidents. You are able to act quickly to stay safe driving because you have a "healthy suspicion" about the other drivers on the road with you. You are not anxious or paranoid about everything that happens but you notice and pay attention to the warning signs that there is a risk of harm because of the actions of another. When you identify the risk, you act on instinct and assume that the risk is real. Your actions avert disaster most of the time.

Maintaining a healthy suspicion about the adults who interact with children in our environments means learning about the behaviors that potentially risky adults exhibit and finding out how to intervene to stop the action. Knowing these potentially risky adult behaviors is the first step in achieving our goal of preventing child sexual abuse. Once we know what behaviors are risky, we must become so familiar with them that they are one of the filters through which we view life. When we can see the warning signs and react appropriately, we can prevent child sexual abuse in many, many cases.

So, the question then becomes, "How do we identify these potentially risky adult behaviors?" As noted in Chapter 3, we begin by going to the source. Child molesters are our best resource for gathering this information. Interviews with molesters, review of cases of molestation and how the grooming process worked and interviews with victims of sexual abuse have helped us identify certain behaviors that should give us pause — behaviors that need to be interrupted because they place everyone in the situation at risk.

These behaviors should raise red flags. They should trigger actions on our part to intervene in situations that might be potentially harmful or even dangerous. These behaviors point to potentially risky adults. They give us clues to help us prevent child sexual abuse. Once we become proficient at recognizing and reacting to these behaviors we can stop risky situations early. That will accomplish two goals. It will interrupt the grooming process of a child molester and, if the person whose behavior is at issue intends no harm, motivate the person to change his or her behavior to eliminate the concern.

The beginning of developing proficiency is gathering information. In the next chapters, we are going to carefully consider some of these potentially risky behaviors (PRB) and begin to learn how to tell the difference between a genuinely caring individual and an adult who is a risk to children. We also will begin to learn how to intervene in risky situations and protect children.

CHAPTER 5

PRB #1:
Always Isolated and Alone

The first Potentially Risky Behavior singles out those people who: **always prefer be alone with children and to isolate children from others.**

Most of society seems to settle on one of two views of people who spend time alone with children. They either see the adult as a caring, nurturing person who is committed to children, or they see the person who spends time alone with children on the job or in a volunteer or ministerial capacity as a pervert who can't be trusted at all. The decision about which view to adopt often is based on whether the person seems to be someone we think of as deserving of trust.

However, "spending time alone" with children is not necessarily a measuring stick for identifying adults exhibiting this PRB and neither is a subjective opinion about whether that person "seems" to be someone who deserves our trust. The key element of concern about this behavior can be seen by applying a completely objective standard to the person's interactions with children. The question to ask is: "Does this person consistently arrange circumstances so that he or she is alone with children in locations where others are not likely to show up or drop by?" If the answer is "yes," do what you need to do to interrupt the behavior. Let the person know this behavior must stop. Once that is accomplished, keep an eye on this person to make sure that this kind of thing does not happen again.

Objectively observing the adult's behavior will help you identify the adult's preferences or desires without relying on your feelings or preconceived notions about the adult as the determining factor. Watch what people do and you are more likely to know whether someone is a potentially risky adult.

Ask yourself questions such as:

- Is this someone who always seems to want to be alone with children or young people?

- Does the person object to other people's participation, or arrange things so no one else can come along?

- Does the person always or almost always schedule appointments — even seemingly legitimate appointments — to take place after everyone else has left the building or on days and at times when no one else will be around?

- Does the person get indignant and/or appear to be offended if you question the scheduling?

- Is this someone who tries to convince children and parents that it is okay for the children to meet them in out-of-the-way places or areas with no windows after hours when no one else is around?

- Does the person making comments intended to make the adult raising questions about the behavior feel guilty about questioning what's happening?

If the answer to any of these questions is "yes" or even "most of the time," this is a potentially risky adult behavior. Exhibiting this behavior does not mean the person is a child molester. It is possible the person simply is arrogant or thoughtless. However, as Dr. Finkelhor points out, one of the elements necessary for sexual abuse to occur is an environment where there is an opportunity for abuse to occur.

That means child molesters need privacy to commit their crimes. These behaviors create an environment of isolation and separation that place children at risk and raise concerns about an adult's intentions.

To answer questions about the behavior of the adults in our children's lives does not compel us to follow people around gathering information. It does, however, require that we pay attention. Paying attention to where and when adults meet with children means taking notice of what is happening. We cannot turn a blind eye to these situations any more than we can ignore public displays of abusive behavior.

Child sexual abuse, and the seduction of children by adults in the environment, is not so easy to see, but it also is not totally hidden from view if we know what to look for. Predators operate in the shadows of life. They deliberately create opportunities for secluding a child and the reasons they give seem valid and reasonable. As a result, it is important for adults to be alert to and observant of the patterns of behavior. A one-time meeting for an extra one-on-one coaching for the school play at 4:00 on Thursday, after all the other teachers and administrators are gone, is not a concern. A regular schedule of private coaching sessions after hours should raise red flags and at least warrant further inquiry.

Only those who prefer to be alone with children in an environment that prohibits monitoring are potentially risky adults. They are not necessarily child molesters but their behavior is risky, and responsible adults must be able to identify the risk and intervene to prevent possible abuse.

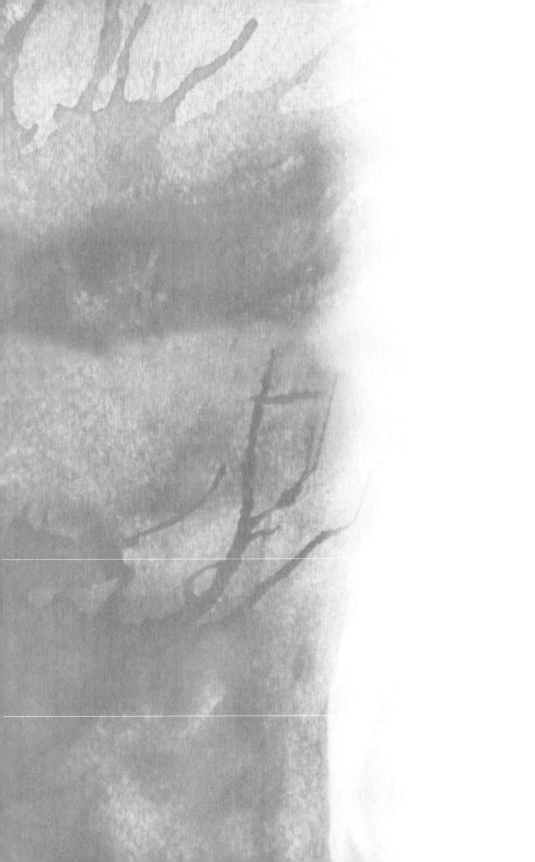

CHAPTER 6

PRB #2:
Gifts That are not "Gifts"

*The second Potentially Risky Behavior raises awareness about those who are: **giving secret "gifts" and expecting something in return.***

Many grandparents and other relatives are guilty of buying gifts without getting permission from parents. Even close friends can fall into this pattern of behavior with children they care about. We see something that reminds us of the child or we know that he or she has been wanting, and we buy it on the spot. That's great — in fact, kids are counting on us to do just that. They know that grandma and grandpa are a soft touch and, frankly, that's exactly how the world is supposed to be.

Buying gifts without permission is not the problem. The problem is *giving* gifts without permission — in particular, giving "secret gifts" and expecting something in return. Responsible grandparents and others who buy gifts without permission must be careful not to give those gifts to children and keep it a secret from parents or guardians. They also must be very clear about the nature of a "gift," and make sure the child understands this also. Failing to do so could set the stage or open the door for a child molester.

People who prey on children use secret gifts for a variety of purposes. None of what they do with these items is actually gift-giving. According to the dictionary, a "gift" is something given voluntarily, without compensation or the expectation of anything in return. When viewed in that light, we can see nothing that is passed on to a child by a molester is really a "gift." Items are not given without expectations attached. They are given for a purpose, with a specific objective in mind. In addition, there are always strings attached. The strings may seem simple and insignificant but they are, nevertheless, strings and attaching them to the item means it is no longer a "gift."

The string can be anything, and it does not necessarily have to be an obvious trade. For example, a request that the person keep the item a secret from someone else may seem like a harmless request. It is not. The fact that the request is made is a *string* attached to the item being passed on and it is no longer a "gift." In that case, the payment is silence.

"Gifts" are often good negotiating tools for parents. However, parents who negotiate cooperation from their children in return for a "present" are not giving a gift, and they should make it clear to children that this kind of a deal is not the same as giving and receiving a gift. It is a more like a business deal, and while those kinds of negotiations have an appropriate place in life, we want children to know the difference between these types of transactions and "gifts."

Sometimes what otherwise would be seen as a bribe is characterized as a "gift." "You can have that iPOD you want if you promise to…" is a great example of the kind of thing that is said to children to manipulate them into doing something we want them to do. If the promise extracted is from parents and the goal is to motivate young people to, for example, bring up their grades, this is classic negotiation. The important thing is not then to call the iPOD a "gift." It is not; it is payment in return for something of value. The parent or guardian wants something and they have decided that the cost of an iPOD is the correct price to pay for what is requested.

Another kind of payment that takes away the gifting of something is the request for something in return such as, "I have a really great gift for you. All you have to do is have dinner with me tomorrow night and I will bring it to you then." That is not a "gift." That, too, is a negotiation.

It may be difficult to admit that many of the "gifts" we have given the children in our lives are not gifts at all. However, if we want to create an environment where an abuser has no real access to our children, we need to broaden our definition of compensation and begin to teach our children how to know the difference — and we need to teach them by example, as well as by providing information.

Compensation can take many forms, and child molesters are very good at creating the appearance that nothing is wrong or inappropriate, while, at the same time making sure their potential victim feels indebted to them. Child molesters find ways to trap children in a situation where the children believe there is no way out.

Some ways child molesters use secret gifts to manipulate and trap children include:

- Buying a child something the child wants but the parents can't afford.

- Letting a child have something that he or she can keep at the molester's home so parents won't know about it.

- Getting the child something that can only be used when with the molester, such as camping equipment or a laptop computer.

- Offering to help the child buy a gift for a parent or sibling — and no one needs to know where it came from or how the child could buy it.

- Giving the child money for something that parents can't afford or refuse to pay for, such as lunch at the mall or treats at the movie.

- Buying kids candy or soda when they don't have the money or parents said "no."

There are three key elements in each of these situations. First, the child is getting something he or she wants that parents either have refused to buy or can't afford to provide. Second, the "gift" is cloaked in secrecy. The agreement between the child and the molester is that the whole transaction is a secret — just between the two of them. The molester may convince the child that the purpose of the secrecy is to protect the parents' pride but the real purpose is to create a wedge between the parents and child resulting in a void that can only be filled by the molester.

The third element is something always is expected in return for the secret gift. The child will be expected to pay for the present sooner or later. It could be that the only thing expected is silence. However, the price may be much, much higher in the future when the "gift" becomes leverage to get the child to engage in sexual activity and keep quiet about it.

One of the challenges parents face is knowing when secret gifts are given. Wouldn't it be nice if child molesters exhibited the warning signs or those behaviors we know are potentially risky right out in the open for everyone to see? It certainly would be easier for us to recognize when a child is being groomed and to take definitive action. The problem is that child molesters often don't exhibit grooming behavior in public.

Child molesters use secret gifts as lures. By their very nature, lures are decoys designed to attract or tempt someone to something that appears attractive but is not what it seems. Fishing lures, for example, are colorful, creative designs that attract fish to a hidden hook. Implanting the hook is the purpose but the allure is the color, composition, and movement of the lure. Its purpose is to dangle something attractive in front of the fish and distract the fish from the hook. The lure makes it easy to catch the prey.

A lure is deceptive. The purpose is to mislead or camouflage the real intent of the item or the action. In order for the deception to work, most of the gift giving that is part of the grooming process must be hidden from view. By that, we mean it must take place away from the watchful eyes of others. Gifts given *as* a secret must also be given *in* secret. As you can see, this makes it difficult to know when someone is exhibiting this PRB. As responsible adults, we must be acutely aware of the power and effectiveness of gift-giving as a grooming technique and pay particular attention to any actions that occur as questionable.

For example, small gifts of food or drink are hard to uncover unless your child tells you about them. The molester gives the secret gift and it is consumed quickly. Parents may need to begin asking questions when children have been out with friends in order to find out what's happening when children and parents are separated.

Also, pay attention to anything new your child has that you did not purchase for him or her. Find out where it came from and who purchased it. Don't be put off by your child's attempts, or those of the adult who purchased the item, to divert your attention from the concerns you have about the situation. If the item was given without your permission, assume it came with strings attached and find out what these are.

Notice if your child is sporting a new shirt, jacket, or backpack. Pay attention to new CDs or a new electronic game. Ask where the item came from, and then follow up and verify the source. If the "new item" is part of a grooming process, finding out about it in the beginning is a real opportunity to thwart the molester's intention, and to protect your child from being trapped in a veil of secrecy.

Be suspicious when someone gives your child a gift without your permission. Let the child's benefactor be on the hot seat and explain his or her actions to you until you are satisfied that there is no ulterior motive. If you are clear that the actions were innocent, make sure the adult knows that giving secret gifts is unacceptable. Set up a practice for making sure that any future gifts are approved by you and truly are gifts.

Anyone who is unwilling to agree to those terms should be eliminated from your child's life. Regardless of the reasons the person gives for giving gifts with strings attached, make sure he or she understands that, in your family, those are not "gifts."

In addition, make sure your children know the difference between gifts and something that has many of the characteristics of a gift but comes with conditions or strings attached. Empower your kids to say "no" to the proposed conditions or to tell you about the offer before they accept, no matter how much they want the item offered. Being indebted to someone can have serious consequences in the future. This is an important lesson for both parents and children.

Let children know anything that comes with conditions is not a gift — though it ultimately may be okay to accept once everyone is clear about the conditions. After careful consideration and discussion, parents and children may decide that the price asked is worth the value received. But, in that case, there is no secrecy and, therefore, no wedge driven between parents and children.

The potentially risky adult behavior that gives rise to concern is giving gifts without permission and telling children to keep the "gift" a secret. When you and your children are clear about the nature of a "gift" and what constitutes a "secret," you can have a powerful impact on the intentions of a child molester that stops them dead in their tracks.

CHAPTER 7

PRB #3:
Too Much Touching

*The next Potentially Risky Behavior looks at those who are: **pushing the limits of appropriate boundaries when touching children.***

Children need human touch. Nurturing touch between parents and children promotes healthy development as well as encouraging attachment and demonstrating affection. The need for nurturing touch does not go away as a child grows up. Hugs, holding hands, and playing games of tag or touch football help children thrive and grow.

Nurturing touch is not limited to contact between parents and children. A pat on the back from a coach or curling up on the sofa with Grandpa to read a book or watch a movie together are also examples of touch that provide a child with a sense of belonging and being loved.

However, not all touching nurtures, and both parents and children need to learn to distinguish between the two. It is important to realize that touching between adults and children is governed by the appropriate boundaries of the relationship. Identifying the nature of appropriate boundaries in different relationships is essential to knowing whether the touch that is occurring is appropriate, or exceeds healthy boundaries.

Setting and honoring boundaries

Everyone is familiar with the idea of boundaries. However, people don't often use the word "boundary" to describe what is happening in a particular situation. For the most part, we act or react automatically to boundary issues.

For example, when someone gets too close to us and we get uncomfortable, we may step away or leave. We deflect questions that are "too personal" by changing the subject or pretending we didn't hear. We are uncomfortable when a clerk at the retail store asks for our phone number or address before ringing up our purchases. In fact, we often give out the information, and immediately we wish we hadn't done so. The minute we give out our phone number we are sure we will start getting a barrage of phone calls from persistent, often annoying telemarketers at inconvenient times.

We usually don't think about these situations as violations of personal boundaries, but they are. They overstep or violate the boundaries or limits that define us and keep us separate from one another. Boundaries promote and preserve personal integrity. They give each of us a clear sense of self and how to function in relation to one another. Boundaries are unique to each individual and they are based on perceptions, personal histories, values, goals, culture, and concerns.

Boundaries are also unique to each relationship. The boundaries between spouses are not the same as the boundaries between friends or siblings. As a result, not all closeness between people is a boundary violation. For example, when someone we care about moves closer to hold our hand or give us a kiss or hug, and we react by moving closer there is no boundary violation. If, on the other hand, someone we just met does the same thing, a boundary violation occurs.

Initially, boundaries are developed by the amount and type of attention people get from their parents. Parents sometimes say or do things that leave children with a distorted view of the boundaries in their relationships. A parent who repeatedly tells a child that his or her actions are "breaking my heart," or says "How could you do this to me?" or reacts in anger when the child doesn't follow the rules, risks leaving the child thinking he or she has the power to determine someone's feelings. A child could use that belief in any number of ways in relationships as they grow up – including to manipulate and control others.

Raising awareness about personal boundaries is the foundation for creating healthy frameworks for relationships. Children need to know they have a right to set boundaries and expect others to honor them. Adults need to keep an eye on the people around them who are interacting with children and intervene when boundaries are being violated or compromised in any way.

A violation of boundaries is determined by the experience of the person whose boundary was breached, not by the intent of the actor. Even an unintended boundary violation is not a justification for leaving someone with the experience of being violated and left open and vulnerable.

When an adult touches a child too much or too intimately, boundary violations can occur. However, knowing that is the case does not necessarily open the door to identifying those touching behaviors that could be too much or too intimate, and it does not help us protect children from predators.

As responsible adults, we need to know about two particular kinds of behaviors that we must become proficient at recognizing in ourselves and in others. The first is conditioning behavior, and the second is risky touching. Conditioning behavior is something we do without realizing the potential damage, and risky touching is something that potentially risky adults may do to break down a child's defenses or as part of the grooming process.

Conditioning behavior

Some behaviors between adults and children are inappropriate simply because of how they impact the child and the environment. Those who regularly interact with other people's children need to take a careful look at all their interactions with children with a particular objective in mind.

Adults who provide care and services to children who are not part of their family through jobs, volunteer activities, friendships, etc. must take care that their interactions with these youngsters do not unintentionally create new openings for child molesters to gain access to children. Child molesters are clever and creative. Among their tricks is finding ways to use our legitimate interactions with children to their advantage. As a result, we need to reexamine all of our interactions with children from two separate perspectives.

When looking at interactions, activities, and communications with children, there are two key questions to ask yourself:

- Could this contact or activity condition children to accept touch that, in other circumstances, might be considered intimate or inappropriate?

- Could this contact or activity condition the community to accept potentially inappropriate or intimate behavior between adults and children?

In a later chapter, we will create a standard of behavior for adults that can help make sure that all of our interactions with children are appropriate. However, to assure that we are part of the solution to make a child's world a safer place, we must re-examine the activities we engage in with children.

To answer the first question, we need to look carefully at our activities with children from a particular perspective. Nothing is wrong with or inappropriate about most of the activities adults engage in with children and, of course, some interactions with family members are subject to different rules. However, certain activities can create an opening or a conduit through which a child molester can gain access to the child. To determine whether a particular activity could allow this to happen, we need to look at the physical interactions we have with children who are not part of our family using two basic criteria for assessing these games and activities. They are:

- Does the activity involve touching between adults and children that could be intimate (even accidentally)?

- Does the activity or contact involve forcing children to touch or be touched in order to continue to participate — or put children in a position of not being able to refuse? This applies even if the touch is non-sexual.

Look carefully at all the games and activities involving adults and children. Make sure there is no part of the activity that could result in children being touched in an intimate way, even if the interaction appears to be accidental.

Among the activities to eliminate between adults and children other than family members are such things as:

- Wrestling and tickling.
- Lengthy embraces.
- Kissing children on the mouth.
- Sitting children or young people over two years of age on your lap.
- Touching a child affectionately in an isolated area of the facility, such as staff only areas or other private areas.
- Sleeping in bed with a child.
- Touching knees or legs of children (except, perhaps, to treat a wound or injury or to assist a young child in getting dressed).
- Giving piggyback rides.

- Compliments that relate to physique or body development.
- Any type of massage given by a child to an adult or by an adult to a child or young person.

No matter what the reason for an interaction of this kind, it is inappropriate, and yet, because the child knows you to be trustworthy or feels that they must comply because of your position of authority, they don't know how to stop it. Regardless of your intentions, this kind of activity can condition children to accept touch that might be intimate from adults they don't know very well.

Conditioning the community

Take time to look at the activities between adults and children from the perspective of an observer. Do the activities involve touching that could condition the adult community to accept certain behaviors between adults and children — even if it could be risky when committed by someone with an evil intent?

For example, if a respected adult in the community begins to engage in rough-housing with little boys in the parish because he wants them to know they are valued. The boys can be conditioned to believe that type of touching is something they should just accept —   and the community can become numb to the fact that it is occurring. In that situation, conditioning has occurred that opens the door for a child molester. In addition, there are some "games" used by Youth Ministers in the past that can have the same results such as "Pass the Lifesaver." In this game, children in a circle each have a toothpick in their mouth and they pass a lifesaver around the circle from person to person. Other games involve sitting in laps and tickling. Although the games may seem harmless, they should be evaluated base on whether they can condition the community to allow possibly inappropriate interactions.

When activities condition the community, the door is opened for a child molester to gain access to children — right in front of caring adults — without arousing suspicion. Maintaining high standards for physical interactions between children and adults in parish, school or organizational activities will dramatically improve the community's ability to protect children.

This does not mean an adult may never touch a child. Children need healthy, nurturing touch from adults in their lives. It means that we all need to pay attention to the kinds of touching we allow or engage in, and think about how it is perceived by others. For example, are we initiating the contact or allowing the child or young person to reach out to us? In one situation, the adult is in control and in the other, the adult is truly following the child's lead. One gives cause for concern about how a child molester might take advantage of the conditioning, and the other acknowledges that children have a say in who touches them.

Evaluating our own behaviors in light of these considerations can help us make sure we are creating an environment where the behavior of someone who is a risk of harm to children is noticed. Eliminating situations that make children vulnerable to the actions of potential child molesters can stop a child molester in his or her tracks.

Be aware of a pitfall

Many of the activities that need review were developed to accomplish a legitimate and important organizational or educational goal. Don't "throw the baby out with the bathwater," so to speak, by eliminating the activity without replacing it with something that accomplishes the goal of supporting and nurturing the child but does not create a risk of harm to children. Creative, caring people can find appropriate ways to nurture healthy development of children without relying on inappropriate touching.

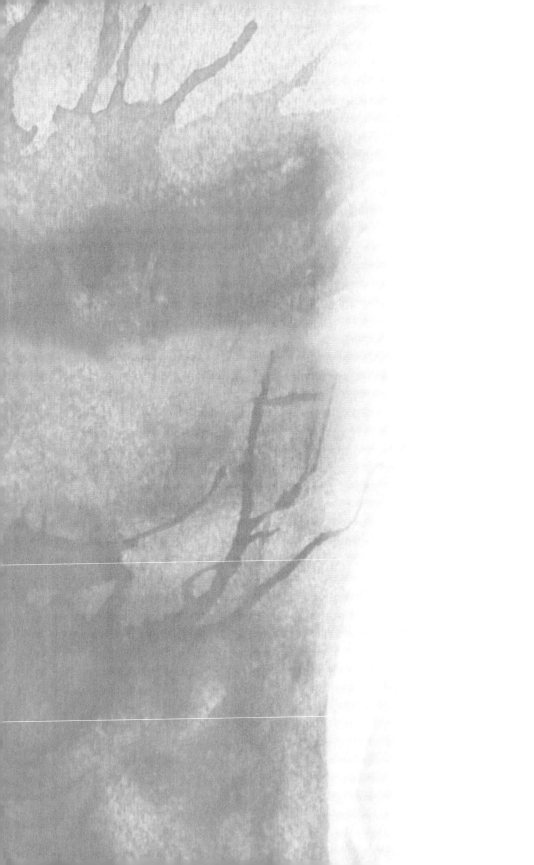

CHAPTER 8

PRB #4
Inappropriately Indulging Children

Our next Potentially Risky Behavior reminds us to watch for: **people who indulge children and allow them to participate in activities their parents would not permit.**

Most dictionary definitions of "indulge" include some version of the phrase "to allow a person to do or have what he or she wishes." Adults who indulge children, even those with no intention to do harm, are exhibiting another potentially risky adult behavior.

Indulging children is something people enjoy doing. Grandparents, aunts and uncles, and others love doting on children. It seems to be their job to provide special events and a fun, relaxed atmosphere without so many rules. In fact, it's expected. It is one of the things children look forward to, and grandparents and other close friends and relatives feel as though they are entitled to do it. In other words, children love it and so do the adults who indulge them.

Being indulged in this way is just part of the magic of being a child. It provides special, unexpected moments of joy for everyone involved, and leaves children with the experience of being special and cared for. However, the joy of these experiences can be short lived. These situations can also be the source of serious problems for both children and parents when the indulgence is kept secret.

No adult, regardless of motive, should indulge a child by allowing the child to do things parents or guardians would not allow them to do without getting permission or at least letting the parents or guardians know what's happening — even when the intent is harmless.

Indulging children by allowing them to do things parents won't let them do, and doing it without parents' knowledge and consent, drives a wedge between parents and their children. This is one of the ways child molesters groom children. This kind of behavior indicates that someone is a risk to children.

One of the problems in this area is that people tend to base their opinion about whether the indulgence is harmful on the thing the children are being allowed to do. For example, most responsible people agree that allowing children to smoke, drink, do drugs, or look at pornography, constitutes destructive indulgence that should be interrupted. Those same people might be surprised that allowing a child to stay up late or eat junk food, without telling parents, is also indulgence. They may see these actions as harmless. After all, they only happen occasionally and these activities are not a harmful. It does not seem like a "big deal." Most of the time it's a treat that accompanies a visit with Grandma and Grandpa, or a special event of some kind.

Child molesters have a different view. Their objective is not to "spoil" a grandchild or a favorite niece or nephew. They are interest in the best avenue for seduction. They indulge children as part of that process.

One of the ways we know that this works is from the child molesters themselves. They repeatedly point to indulging children as a way to gain trust and establish relationships with children.

They also say that a pivotal factor in identifying the children most vulnerable to seduction is to recognize those that come from tightly controlled environments where children live within strict, narrow boundaries. They indulge children in small, seemingly insignificant ways, as part of the grooming process. The indulgence may go unnoticed by the adults but it is a real prize to the children. Children crave the extra attention and they thrive on the tidbits of freedom the offender offers.

In these situations, it is also easier for the molester to convince the child to keep silent. Once a cycle of silence is introduced, the offender uses that as leverage to establish and maintain a pattern of silence and secrecy. In this way, the adult makes sure future activities and actions are surrounded by a wall of secrecy.

Adults need to pay attention to these small indulgences. Notice when an adult provides junk food snacks to children who are only allowed to eat healthy food. Pay attention to the times you overhear an adult say something like, "It's okay. It won't matter just this once." Be alert to times when adults give children permission to do anything that parents have objected to or are opposed to. It may be nothing at all. It may just be poor judgment on the part of a well-meaning adult. Or it may be the initial contacts of a child molester who is laying the groundwork for future harm.

Of course, if this is the only sign you see, find out whether the parents already gave their permission. Don't just assume that the person is behaving in a risky manner. It is possible the parents know what's happening and the kids know this is not something that is a "secret" from parents. If so, there is no problem. If not, your inquiry will raise a red flag and alert the parents to what's going on without any accusations of wrongdoing.

Indulging children is one of the joys of being a grandparent or a favorite aunt or uncle. Being open and honest about it protects the children and the adults in their lives from harm.

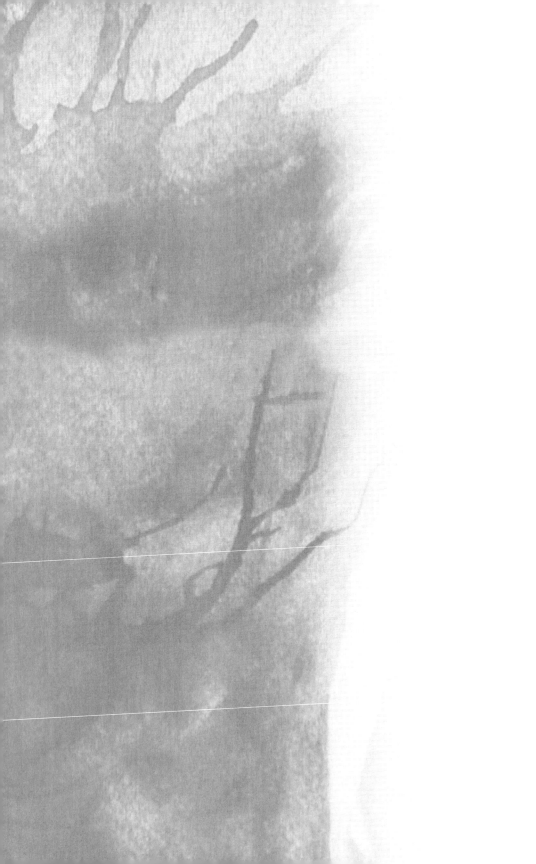

CHAPTER 9

PRB #5
"No Rules" Apply

*Another Potentially Risky Behavior that requires attention is: **people who think they don't have to follow the rules.***

Many people have commented that a person who molests children obviously is not in their right mind. Although that is clear to those who would never consider sexual activity with a child, those who molest children do not have the same view of the situation. They often believe it is okay to love a child sexually and that children love it, too.

The net effect of this attitude is that child molesters often operate in the world as if the rules that govern society do not apply to them. It isn't necessarily that they deliberately disregard the rules; it is more like they just don't think the rules are for them. For example, one child molester who was interviewed about how he was apprehended talked about the activity that triggered his arrest for taking pictures of naked children in his home. It was obvious that his view of the situation was quite different from that of the rest of society.

Picture-taking usually is harmless. The world is full of computer files, photo albums, and boxes in closets that overflow with the abundance of our children's lives in pictures, and pictures of us and our families as children. However, this child molester was taking pictures of naked ten-year-old boys in his home. During the interview it became clear that he believed the rules of society did not apply to him. He seemed a bit surprised at the outrage that the pictures produced. After all, according to him, the boys were just jumping on the bed and running around, and there were no sexual poses so the fact that they were naked should not have been a problem. As a result of this distorted thinking, he took the film to a local business to get the pictures developed. The developer, being of "right" mind and acutely aware of the rules of society where adults and children are concerned, immediately called in law enforcement, and the child molester's activities were discovered. This is one real-life example of how the thinking of a child molester is distorted and leaves them operating as if they don't have to go by the same rules that apply to the rest of society.

A person who believes it is okay to have sexual relations with a child obviously is not thinking straight, but the more we look into the behavior of offenders, the more we realize their outlook on most things is "no rules apply." They don't think they need to follow standard policies and procedures. They don't think they need to do things the way society dictates.

Another example of the attitude of "no rules apply" is evident in the screening process for potential employees or volunteers to work with children. In a later chapter, we will discuss the proper elements of a screening program for applicants for jobs and volunteer positions working with children. However, many of those jobs require that all applicants undergo a criminal background check. This requirement does not always stop a sex offender from applying. They think it will all work out for them anyway. So some of them apply for the jobs and sign an authorization for a review of their criminal records even knowing that a thorough review will uncover their history of sex offenses. Through their distorted thinking, they do not appear to be worried. Some think the very fact that they signed the authorization will be enough to satisfy the organization and no real background check will occur. Who in their "right mind" would authorize a criminal background check knowing that it would show a conviction as a sex offender?

Or, they may sign because they believe the organization will actually not do a comprehensive nationwide search. After all, the cost of a federal search or research that covers all 50 states is much too much for most organizations to bear — or so the molester thinks. If the sex offender is living in Oklahoma, and all his or her offenses were committed in Delaware, a local criminal background check will be clean.

Ironically, these two schools of thought have been used by organizations to justify deciding not to go through with the background checks at all. Some managers have convinced themselves that a signed authorization is proof enough of a clean record. So they decide to avoid the cost of the background check. Others decide the cost of more comprehensive checks is unnecessary because of the same signed authorization. Checking the local records is evidence of a good-faith effort to conduct criminal background checks. Child molesters count on this "logic" to gain access to children through positions that normally would be closed to them.

Child molesters are manipulative and calculating in their efforts to gain access to children. Those of us who do not think that way may have a difficult time imagining what someone with predatory objectives might think or do. Knowing that child molesters do not think the rules of society apply to them can help us realize when risky situations arise.

In addition to the distorted thinking that sometimes causes molesters to operate outside the rules, those who have this attitude often disregard standard policies and procedures. For example, if the organization has a policy that requires two adults to stay at events until all the children have been picked up, the potential child molester will offer to stay alone and encourage everyone else to leave. He or she often will say things like, "I have known these kids for years. Their parents are always late. They won't mind if I am the only one here when they come." Or they might say, "The parents will be here in a few minutes. It'll be okay. I know you have things to do." However the conversation goes, it is intended to convince the other adults that the policies and procedures put in place to protect both the children and adults don't apply in the situation and should be overlooked by everyone.

This subtle attempt to undermine the rules or divert people from following the policies and procedures is just one way child molesters are attempting to rewrite the rules or suspend their application. Other attempts are more blatant and direct but the underlying justification is the belief that the rules of society do not apply to child molesters.

They walk into children's bathrooms and bedrooms un-invited and unannounced. They may act as if it is an "ac-cident" but the objective is to catch children off-guard. After all, the rules of decency and respect for boundaries aren't for them. A closed door does not mean "respect privacy" so an intimate moment is not off limits. They may apologize for the intrusion but that does not mean they won't do it again and again and keep apologizing. They intend to break down the child's resistance by breaking the rules and using these "accidents" to push the limits.

Many individuals who molest children are so convinced that not only do the rules not apply to them, but the rules are actually wrong that they are actively working toward a new paradigm for society. They want society to change the rules to allow sex between adults and children. This is the ultimate example of the degree to which child molesters are not in their "right" mind and operate outside the norms of society. They believe that society should relate to sex be-tween adults and children as normal.

There are organizations actively working to promote this idea. Organizations such as Sex Offender Support and

Education Network, also known as SOSEN or S.O.S.E.N., SO Clear, and Roar4Freedom, actively and aggressively promote a political agenda that seeks to redefine the rules of society to include the behavior of sex offenders and label it as acceptable. In fact, the stated goal of SOSEN is the elimination of the Sex Offender Registry and all harsh laws against sex offenders. They fail to see their behavior as aberrant. Society must be wrong.

Through these organizations and others like them, convicted offenders and some members of their families also are working to convince society that child molesters are just people who were in the wrong place at the wrong time and did nothing to deserve the conviction or the label "sex offender."

Believing and operating as if the rules of society do not pertain to them is a potentially risky behavior. It can manifest itself in a multitude of ways. In addition to those discussed here, be aware of people who always think it is okay to arrive late to programs, seminars, or meetings, or to leave early, or people who seem to think that things should be modified or revised to suit their particular needs or desires. Notice whether these are just arrogant, self-centered or careless adults or if they also exhibit other potentially risky adult behaviors. Don't be afraid to raise questions about any behavior that occurs to you as odd or makes you uncomfortable. Trust your instincts. Pay attention to situations that make you uneasy and don't talk yourself out of the feeling. Too many times, adults have commented, after a child was harmed, that something about the situation made them uncomfortable but they did not know what to do or whether their concerns were justified. Anything that raises your concerns or gives you an uneasy feeling should be taken seriously.

Realize that it takes courage to act on those uneasy feelings, particularly when you think you know the person well or have developed a level of trust for the person or their family. Speaking up, taking notice, and trusting your own instincts is a courageous act. Also remember the famous quote from Ambrose Redmoon and trust that the welfare of our children is more important than your fear or anxiety about speaking up or embarrassing someone else.

> *Courage is not the absence of fear, but rather the judgment that something else is more important than fear.* — AMBROSE REDMOON

CHAPTER 10

PRB #6
Going it Alone

*Another Potentially Risky Behavior points us toward adults who: **isolate children in places where others have no chance to observe their time together.***

One of the four elements necessary for child sexual abuse to occur is an opportunity for the offender to be with the child in a secluded place. Child molesters need to be alone with a child for a period of uninterrupted time in order to commit their crimes. Most of us have witnessed situations that we would consider physically or emotionally abusive in a grocery store, a park, or at a community or family event. Sexual abuse is different. Privacy is required. Therefore, the molester makes a concerted effort to be alone with children.

In fact, child molesters are very good at managing to seclude children in ways that may seem legitimate or un-avoidable — at least on the surface. One of the reasons this may be difficult to distinguish is that there are many legiti-mate reasons for an adult to be alone with a child.

Therapy or counseling sessions, music lessons, and tu-toring are often one-on-one, and the privacy maintained in these sessions is important for the goals to be achieved. In addition to structured, appropriate, one-on-one events, adults sometimes find themselves alone with a child or young person unexpectedly. Without other evidence, other PRBs, or other concerns, these situations are not risky.

So, how do adults know when something is okay, and when what's happening is a warning sign that something is not right? Once again, instincts are an important place to start. If it does not feel right, then something about the situation needs to be changed or addressed. However, there are also a couple of ways this warning sign shows up in the grooming process. Child molesters discourage other people from participating in events or activities. They also manage or schedule their time with children in ways that assure privacy.

Pay attention to people who aggressively or strongly discourage others from participating or being involved. Some activities don't take several people to accomplish. The potentially risky adult is the one who always and only volunteers for those tasks and usually with the same child or children.

Intervening in this situation is easy. Just make sure that either the responsibility for those activities rotates among all the adults involved with the group, or there are two adults present at all times regardless of the need for more than one to complete the task.

Also, be alert to the person who always seems to volunteer for tasks that only require one adult or who sets up one-on-one meetings with children when no one else is around. For example, be wary of the coach or music teacher who wants to provide specialized coaching with the children after school, but always schedules the appointment for 4:15 p.m., after all the other teachers have left the building.

Being alone with children does not automatically make someone suspect. However, the way these sessions happen can give rise to concerns. Adults who genuinely care about children and have no intention of doing harm rarely think of the risks they are creating for themselves and the children they are with. It may never occur to them that someone else might find the situation questionable or risky. As adults, it is important for us speak up and point out risky situations to our colleagues and other adults in the environment.

It is also up to each of us to examine our relationships and activities with children to make sure we are creating an "open door" attitude. Let others know that you will be alone with a child and invite them to drop by during the lesson or session. Make sure you meet in places with no doors or with windows in the door, and then be sure to situate yourself in such a way that you are fully visible to anyone who walks by. Invite parents or guardians to sit in on lessons or to come early or drop by unannounced.

These kinds of actions demonstrate that the intention of the adult is wholesome and genuine. Those who try to convince others to stay away, no matter how sincere their comments, are behaving in a questionable and risky manner. Once again, these behaviors must not be allowed to go on without comment. They need to be interrupted. The adult needs to know the nature of the concern and find a way to alleviate the concern by changing his or her behavior. If the risky behavior does not change, stop the adult's interactions with the child. Take the child out of the situation and find another coach, teacher, or therapist. There are many who are anxious to care for children in an environment that does not raise concerns. Find someone you can trust completely with the child or children in your life.

Finally, the child molester also "secludes" a child through intimidation, fear, and isolation. There are instances when a child has been molested in the same car with other adults, on a bus full of students, or even in the same room, perhaps at the dinner table. In those situations, the child was already secluded from others by the intimidation and manipulation. When a child is secluded psychologically, the abuse can occur anywhere. Awareness of this fact should be the catalyst for parents to pay special attention to the adults discussed in the next chapter, those who seem to be "the answer" to their prayers.

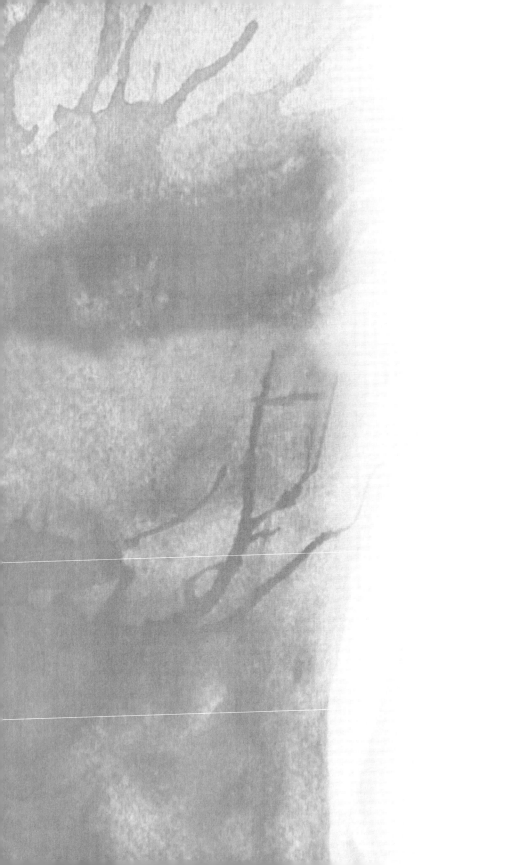

CHAPTER 11

PRB #7
Being "the Answer"

*Perhaps the most difficult Potentially Risky Behavior to identify is: **adults who always seem to be the ones available to help parents manage busy schedules and hectic lives.***

Adults who repeatedly offer their assistance to busy families are usually welcomed with open arms by today's busy families. Parents and guardians usually jump at the offer of help. They see the support as relief and rarely think to examine the motivation behind the person who always seems to offer a helping hand.

Child molesters ingratiate themselves into the lives of potential victims and their families as an essential part of the grooming process. It is critical to their objectives that they find a way to resolve any of the parents' concerns or uneasiness as quickly as possible. Child molesters must have the trust and support of the parents, guardians, and other adults important in the life of a child to gain the kind of access to children needed to accomplish their objectives.

The "answer" for parents

One way child molesters groom adults and gain their trust is by providing support and help to parents and guardians in times of stress or overwhelm. A potential child molester takes steps to become "the answer" for parents or guardians.

This person repeatedly volunteers to provide rides to soccer practice, steps in to tutor the child with math problems, mentors a child in need of guidance, and offers to provide babysitting. He or she looks for openings to offer services and support that busy parents need. They look for people who are spread thin with family and work responsibilities or those with unwieldy schedules and too little time for all the things that need to get done in a day or a week. They befriend these parents and guardians and step in to provide relief. However, the relief is always in the form of activities that involve the children and exclude the parents or situations that allow the molester to separate the child from the parent or diminish the parents' role.

Child molesters need to find ways to ingratiate themselves in the lives of families and establish trusting relationships with parents and guardians carefully and without seeming obvious. They must be thoughtful and methodical throughout this process. If not, responsible adults will see through their attempts to get close to children.

From time to time, after we find out that a child has been molested by someone we know or by a family member, we wonder how this could happen. How could parents be so gullible? How could responsible adults not see what this person was doing to their child? After all, a responsible adult would never allow another person to separate them from their own child. There are two problems with this reaction. First, we are blaming the victims, rather than focusing our attention on the criminal and how the crime was committed. Second, we don't realize the degree of cunning and manipulation that has been used by the child molester to accomplish his or her objective.

It is always important to provide parents with the tools they need to be the best parents they can be. We want parents to raise healthy, well-adjusted children. Blaming parents for children being victimized will not accomplish this goal. When we look to the parents or guardians as if they are somehow lax or irresponsible in this process, we are missing the thing that can really make a difference. Parents and guardians are sucked into the web of the child molester. They are duped into trusting someone who is not trustworthy. Blaming them for being blindsided by someone they grew to trust over time is not going to help. They are placing the blame on themselves already.

What can make a difference is keeping our eyes on all the adults in the environment who interact with children. It is critical that each of us maintains a healthy suspicion about all the adults who interact with our children. Recognizing behavioral warning signs puts the emphasis and attention where it belongs — on the potential abuser.

When someone appears to be too eager to step in for parents or too available to take care of the children, speak up. Call the situation to the attention of parents and guardians. Let them know that something is not right and they should interrupt the pattern.

The "answer" for children

One of the most effective ways a child molester breaks down a child's resistance is to agree with a child when the parents say "no." A child molester can establish an immediate rapport with a child by simply saying, "I can't believe your Mom said you could not do that. If I was your parent I would let you do it." In that moment, the child has an adult ally, someone who is perceived to be on the child's side. There is now a trusted adult who agrees that the child's request is reasonable and responsible.

If you consider how much of the time parents and children are at odds over a child's request to do something the parents object to, you can see how vulnerable children are to the advances of a child molester. They agree with children.

They speak to them on their level. They take interest in the things children are interested in. They offer to go to bat for them with parents, guardians, coaches, bullies, or anyone who is at odds with the child.

They listen. They take time to find out what the child is interested in and what the child dreams about. Then they learn about these things so they can use this information to get closer to the child and build relationship and trust.

They find out where children are struggling and make themselves available to rescue children from difficult situations. They offer to tutor children struggling in school or to provide one-on-one coaching for a child who wants to play soccer but is not making progress.

In other words, they make it their business to find out what the child needs or wants, and then they become the answer. They do whatever it takes to meet the child's needs. They look for ways to give the child what he or she wants — even when they know that parents don't or won't approve. In this way, they not only support the child in doing something or learning something that the child wants or needs to know, but they manipulate the situation in order to establish and seal a bond with the child and build trust into the relationship. The child comes to trust and rely on this person, and the child molester uses that relationship to his or her advantage.

Molesters also often single out children who are isolated or seem lonely. They see children who are ostracized by classmates as particularly good targets. Young people who have few — or no — friends are also high on the molester's hit list. For example, molesters who see summer camps or boarding schools as fertile ground for locating potential victims have no trouble identifying the vulnerable, lonely camper quickly. These adults will begin immediately to befriend the youngster who is unusually homesick or doesn't seem to fit in with the other children. They will offer comfort, support, and special attention while they find out what he or she wants or needs to feel special. All this is part of the game of grooming the child and becoming someone the child trusts and relies on. Once that bond is formed, once the child molester has become the answer for the child, the seduction begins in earnest and the child experiences being trapped. For the child, there is no way out. The only thing to do is live through it.

Another way the molester gains access to children is through his or her own children. Although research tells us that approximately 29 percent of the sexual assaults on children are committed by members of their own biological families, another 60 percent are committed by people known and trusted by the children and families. (Russell, et al.)

Obviously, some child molesters victimize their own children. In fact, it is safe to say that most child molesters victimize their own children in some way. However, not all of them *molest* their own children. Some never touch their own children sexually, but how they treat their children can only be characterized as abusive. For example, they use their children as bait for gaining access to other children. They use their own children to lure other children over to their house. They use their own children as evidence of their concern for kids and to convince other parents of their own trustworthiness. The scars left by this deliberate manipulation, although certainly different from the damage done by child sexual abuse, can be deep and lasting.

Whether the molester is becoming the answer for parents, children, or both, it is important for everyone in the community to pay attention to those who seem willing to step in and take over for busy parents or pick out certain vulnerable children to befriend. Simply interrupt the flow — interject yourself into the situation and come between the potential molester and the children and families that are caught in the apparent grooming process. If nothing is wrong, there likely will not be a reaction. If something more is happening, you will be an unwelcome intrusion — but you will know that your observations and actions are making a difference.

CHAPTER 12

PRB #8:
Cultivating Relationships with Children

*Another Potentially Risky Behavior to notice is: **people who use legitimate skills for cultivating relationships with children to gain access to potential victims.***

Have you ever noticed that there are some adults who seem to communicate more easily with children than others do? They talk the same language as the children and speak at their level. Sometimes this is simply an indicator that the person has taken the time and put in the work to learn how to talk with children in a way that makes a difference. Good teachers, effective caring youth ministers, and others who work with children are among those who learn to communicate with children in this way. Their objective is to do their job well and provide what is needed to help children learn in a healthy environment.

Others who exhibit these behaviors have a different purpose. Some use their ability to get close to children as a tool for establishing relationships and gaining access to children. They use their skills to break down a child's defenses and encourage the child to trust them, even though they are not the least bit trustworthy. These adults bring their ability to communicate with children on their level to bear on their objective of cultivating trusting relationships with children.

There are a few elements to watch for as you consider whether the behavior of the adult is that of a genuinely caring person with a commitment to children or someone with a wicked or reprehensible agenda. Start by looking to see whether the person has a good reason for acting in a child-like manner. Is this a teacher or counselor who is working to create a relationship with a child for the purpose of providing support and care? Even if the answer is "yes," your job is not over.

Caring adults must keep an eye on these interactions and watch for signs that the adult is trying to isolate or seclude the child. This is definitely a situation that requires maintaining a "healthy suspicion." Notice whether the adult stops talking or interrupts the activity when another adult shows up to join in. Pay attention to the nature of the interactions between the adult and the child. Watch for evidence of intimacy and attempts to exclude others, both adults and children. Notice whether the adult seems to single out one child for special attention.

Also, listen to the adult's explanation or comments about what is happening if someone asks. Does the person appear to be making excuses for his or her behavior or trying to convince others that there is nothing wrong? Notice whether the adult is making light of the situation or tying to ridicule your concern. Let them know your objective is simple: protecting children and perpetuating a safe environment for everyone.

Another thing to consider is whether the adult is engaging other adults or inviting others to participate. Those with nothing to hide and no harmful agenda will find the participation of others to be desirable. They will encourage others to join in the activities and act in a childlike manner.

Just like many responsible, caring adults, child molesters also take time to find out what children like and what they are interested in. Again, when observing this behavior, it can be hard to distinguish between those with a genuine interest in children and those who are only interested in cultivating a relationship with the child that leads to a sexual relationship. As with many other warning signs, adult observers should keep an eye on adults who express an interest in getting to know more about the things that children are interested in. Take note of any attempt to seclude or isolate children or to single any child out for special attention, particularly by an adult who seems to want to keep the child away from others. These actions, coupled with an intense interest in something the child likes, should be warning signs that the adult involved poses a risk of harm to children.

One other common behavior that potential child molesters exhibit could be referred to as "being agreeable"; in other words, adults who agree with children when they are upset with their parents. "No" is a word children do not like to hear. They want what they want, when they want it. They are frustrated by answers like "maybe" or "we'll see" from parents or other responsible adults. They prefer definitive answers and they want the answer to be "yes."

A child who is at odds with parents because a request was refused is particularly vulnerable to the advances of a potential child molester. An adult who sides with the child against the parents is exhibiting a PRB.

Adults are responsible for observing every adult in the environment to notice and interrupt PRBs exhibited by anyone. Adults who are really effective communicating with children and cultivating close relationships with children may be genuinely caring adults with a gift for nurturing children as they grow up. We want to encourage those people in their commitment. However, behavior that crosses the line from open and caring to manipulative and divisive is unacceptable and must be broken up. That can only happen if conscientious adults are paying attention.

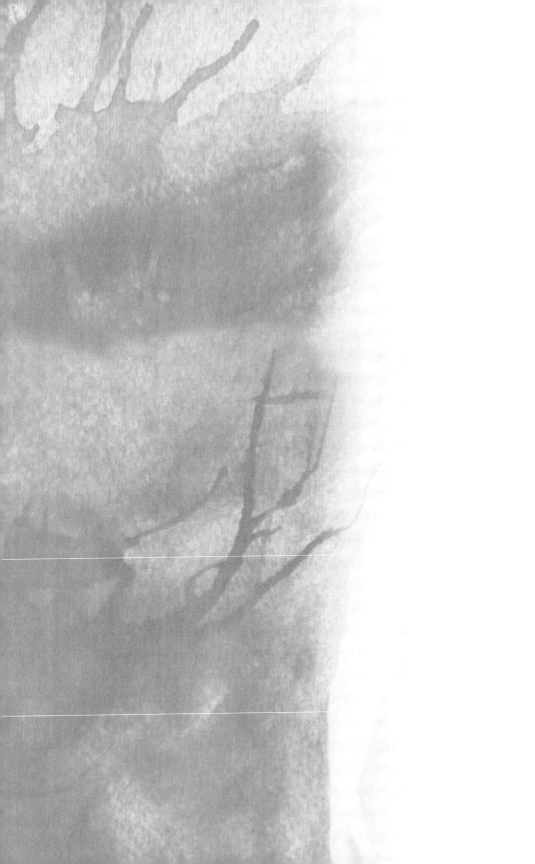

CHAPTER 13

PRB #9:
Sexual Language and Adult Materials

*A difficult Potentially Risky Behavior to find out about is: **adults who use sexually explicit language around children and show them pornography.***

Sexual jokes, sexual language, and adult materials play a more substantial role in the seduction of children than one might imagine. It may be that looking at pornography stimulates the desires of the molester. It may be that using sexual language with and showing pornographic pictures to children is one of the ways the molester initiates and reinforces the world of secrecy with the child. It may be a tool used by the molester to provoke the child into being aroused sexually or for some other purpose.

Regardless of the specific purpose for which sexual language and pornography are employed, we need to realize that the use of pornography and sexually explicit language is a significant part of the grooming process. Engaging in these activities is a warning sign that the person is a child molester or a potential child molester. In fact, one study conducted by the United States Postal Inspection Service discovered that 80 percent of those who purchased child pornography were actively molesting children. These activities are not just about looking at pictures; they are behavioral indicators that someone is a potential child molester or already is engaging in child sexual abuse.

Besides being used to stimulate the molester's own sexual desires, showing pornography to children has several different purposes. First, the pictures are sometimes used to attempt to arouse the child sexually. Molesters show children pictures of both adult and child pornography to see whether the pictures, produce a sexual response from the child. In addition, they use the child's reaction as a gauge for how to go forward with what they want. A mild reaction to sexually explicit material may be seen by a potential child molester as a "green light" for the next step in the seduction process. A stronger reaction will cause the potential molester to slow down and lay more groundwork before moving on in the process.

A second use of pornography in the grooming process is to break down barriers. Children know that sexual activity is not appropriate for children. They know their parents, guardians, or caregivers would be upset about them seeing this material — even if they don't fully understand why it is a problem. Viewing pornography with someone they trust makes the activity seem more acceptable. In addition, the molester uses this activity to let the child know what is expected. It is another example of the old adage, "Pictures speak louder than words."

Showing children pornography, telling sexual jokes, and making sexually-explicit comments reduce a child's inhibitions. These activities and conversations, particularly with someone the child has come to know and trust and who is also trusted by the child's parents or family, give the child a false impression both about the nature of the material and the appropriateness for them to look at it. The intention is to convince the child that sexual activity between adults and children is acceptable and normal. The child's instincts are challenged and just like most adults, the child begins to balance the uneasy feeling about these activities with the feelings of trust they have toward the molester. In the confusion, the winner is often the manipulative adult.

It will not be easy for parents, guardians, or other caring adults to discover whether pornography is being shown to children by others. The best way to know is to listen carefully to what children say and to watch what they do. Do they make inappropriate comments about sexual issues? Is their language about sexual matters older than their years? Do they seem to know things that they could or should not know about body parts or sexual activity?

When children make comments that indicate they have seen or heard inappropriate sexual references, ask questions until you find out the source of the information. The child may be reluctant to speak to you because he or she knows you will be upset about what happened. Let the child know that although some material is for "adults only," the child will not be in trouble for looking at the pictures or videos that someone else showed them. Let them know there is a difference between seeing something or looking at a book someone leaves lying around, and actively going out to find this material. Children need to know, even if they have been told that looking at these kinds of pictures, videos, or TV shows is wrong, that seeing pornography intentionally shown to them by someone else is not going to get them in trouble.

One of the most effective ways we can interrupt the possible impact of pornography and sexually-explicit language is to teach our children that they can tell us if someone shows them "adult" material or uses sexual language with them and they won't be in trouble for seeing the material or hearing the jokes and comments.

As adults, we might have a number of different reactions to someone who did those things in our presence — but we would not automatically think we were bad people just because someone else did something we considered in bad taste. Children who are told that pornography is bad have only that information to rely on when someone shows them sexually explicit material or tells a sexual joke. All they know is that they were told it is wrong. They are so literal in their thinking, they go right to an assumption that they will be in trouble because they heard or saw something they weren't supposed to see. It gets worse if they found themselves intrigued by what they saw, if they had some sort of physical reaction to the pictures, or if they laughed at the jokes. They are not bad children because any of these reactions happened, and they need to know that, too. Let them know they can speak up and check things out with parents, guardians, or others who truly care about them without risking the possibility of being punished for doing something they know they weren't supposed to do.

The responsibility of parenting includes establishing boundaries for children and then teaching them the difference between a deliberate violation of those boundaries by them and someone else drawing them into a situation or tricking them into doing something that goes beyond the limit. Remind children that adults should know better than to subject children to pornography or to use sexually explicit language around children. The kids need to know that, if that happens, it is not their fault. They need to be empowered to speak up and tell someone what happened.

CHAPTER 14

PRB #10
Collecting Memorabilia

One Potentially Risky Behavior that should be a big red flag for everyone is: **adults who collect pictures and other memorabilia about children in their environments.**

In today's electronic world, virtually everyone with a cell phone can take pictures and record video at a moment's notice. Most of these cell phone images are the result of spontaneous situations or experiences someone wants to record for future reference. An unexpected experience or event or a special moment preserved for posterity makes most of us appreciate the cell phone's photography capabilities. For the child molester, however, the ability to take pictures with a phone means he or she can collect hundreds, even thousands, of pictures of children, and with everyone watching and thinking nothing of it.

For years, law enforcement has made us aware of one of the most interesting and sinister behaviors exhibited by child molesters. In many cases, when a molester is arrested, a search of his or her belongings reveals journals, photo albums, and/or videos that chronicle their victims and the history of abuse they have committed. Sometimes there are other memorabilia and, in many cases, the photo albums and videos include children they do not know or pictures they downloaded from websites of all kinds.

Parents, grandparents, and others take pictures of their children all the time. As a result, it often seems "normal" for adults to be taking pictures of children at events around the school or community. However, taking pictures of other people's children without permission or purpose is a PRB and should be interrupted.

Remember, child molesters think they love the children they molest. They convince themselves that the children are willing participants in the sexual activities and sometimes even blame the children for "coming on to" them as a justification for their behavior. As a result, these journals and photo albums are, for the child molester, scrapbooks of memories of the special children in their lives.

In addition, some molesters restrict their interactions with children to gathering and obsessing over photos and videos. They "pretend" that the children in the pictures are part of their lives and they use the photographs to seek sexual gratification of their own needs.

No matter why an adult wants or keeps photos, journals, and videos of children other than their own or those they have been asked to photograph, it is a PRB. No one should take pictures of your children or the children around you without permission from parents, guardians, or those responsible for creating photo journals of events or activities.

Policies that prevent posting pictures of children on school websites, or allowing anyone other than authorized photographers to take pictures at special events or activities, can minimize this behavior — if the policy is enforced. Parents, guardians, and other responsible adults should pay attention to those who are taking pictures of children and make sure they are authorized to make video records of the participants. If not, tell them to stop and report them to those in authority. Ask them for any and all records of photos of your children, and follow up to make sure you get the CDs, memory sticks, prints, negatives, videos, and computer records of unauthorized photos of your children. If the person refuses, contact the authorities and let them know what is happening.

This behavior is easily overlooked. However, you know whether you gave anyone else permission to take pictures of your child. If you did not and the person in charge of the event did not authorize the person to take candid photos of the activities, take the action necessary to make sure your children and others participating in the program or activity are protected.

If you meet someone who keeps journals or photo albums of children for no good reason, let those in charge know what is happening and make sure the one taking pictures is clear that this is unacceptable behavior and has been reported to authorities.

Photo journals that chronicle the lives of our children and grandchildren are very special. As they grow up, we can remember special occasions and family events that will never come again. Paying attention when others are taking pictures or filming videos without our permission helps us preserve the special nature of these journals and albums by avoiding the possibility that pictures will be used for some other purpose that degrades, humiliates, or objectifies children.

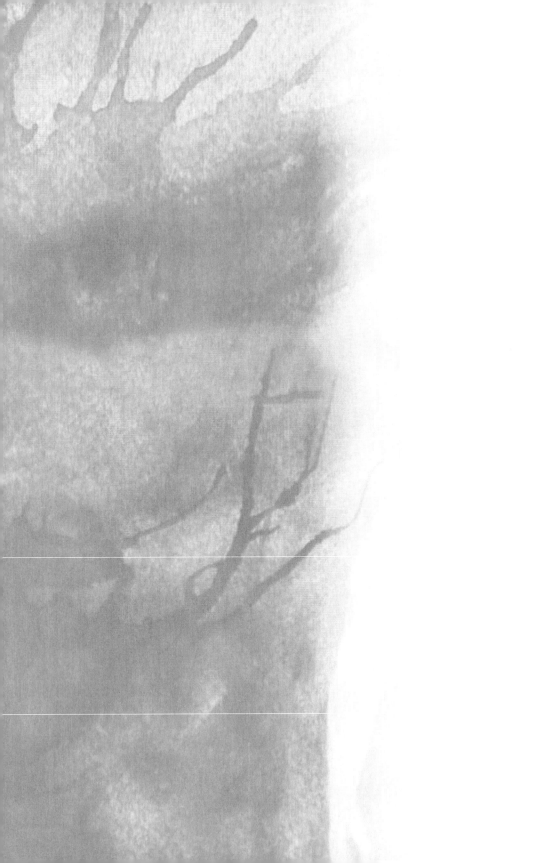

CHAPTER 15

The Internet –
Different and Similar
Behaviors

Every day there seem to be new, unexpected threats to our children's safety cropping up. Cell phones with cameras, Internet chat rooms, MySpace, webcams and other breakthroughs in technology provide exciting, new, faster avenues of communication that also bring new risks that were unheard of and unimagined just a few years ago. Threats from technology often take center stage in the media. Report after report demonstrates the cunning used by predators in their attempts to gain access to children. With so much media attention on the use of technology by child molesters, the tendency is to think we need to redirect adults' attention to finding ways to stop predators that are using technology to gain access to our children.

Parents, guardians, and other adults need to learn about the new tools available to predators. Adults also must be as tenacious and inventive as child molesters in their efforts to discover ways to protect children. However, while these new technological tools provide expanded access, the warning signs remain. No matter how a child molester gains access to a child, the basic behavioral warning signs of adults who pose a threat or risk to children do not change.

Knowing the behavioral warning signs of potentially risky adults is essential to our efforts to protect our children.

Always alone in out-of-the-way places.

Remember that potentially risky adults manage their time with children in ways that leave them alone with children when others are not likely to drop in. Child molesters want to make sure their interactions with children are uninterrupted by other adults and children. In face-to-face encounters family members creep into bedrooms long after the house is asleep. Teachers and coaches meet alone with children after school when no one else is around.

Internet predators are no different. They just find unique ways to be "alone" with children online. They contact children after school, when they are home alone. Children are particularly vulnerable during this time. Child molesters sign-on to chat rooms or social websites and pretend to be about the same age as the child. They seduce the child into a private chat room and make sure their online conversations are "private." They also use technological tools that eliminate the ability of others to listen in. Using these tools, they get children alone and in an out-of-the-way place on the information superhighway.

Gives gifts that are not "gifts."

Whether the child molester is seducing the child in person or through the Internet, gifts are part of the grooming process. The gifts may be related to technology or they may be other kinds of gifts. Webcams and telephones with Internet access are just two examples of the technology-related gifts that predators give. As with other gifts that are not really "gifts," these items come with strings attached. Webcams, for example, give predators a look at children, their homes, and even their private rooms. If predators are able to convince a child to meet in person, they often come with other gifts such as perfume, flowers, or lingerie, or expensive items that the child's parents cannot afford or refuse to purchase.

Indulging children

Through advances in technology, child molesters of all kinds have a new and effective tool for ensnaring children in a web of secrecy. On the Internet, they lure children into activities that parents would forbid and they let them do things parents would find objectionable. Internet predators use the child's desire to be on the Internet — even if parents say "no" — to trap children in a web of secrecy and drive a wedge between children and their parents or guardians.

The potentially risky behaviors of adults who are a threat to children show up in virtually every case of child molestation. The vehicle for contacting children may be school, church, soccer, friends, family, or the Internet. Regardless of the means used to gain access, the behavioral warning signs are the same. Knowing these signs is the best way to prevent child sexual abuse.

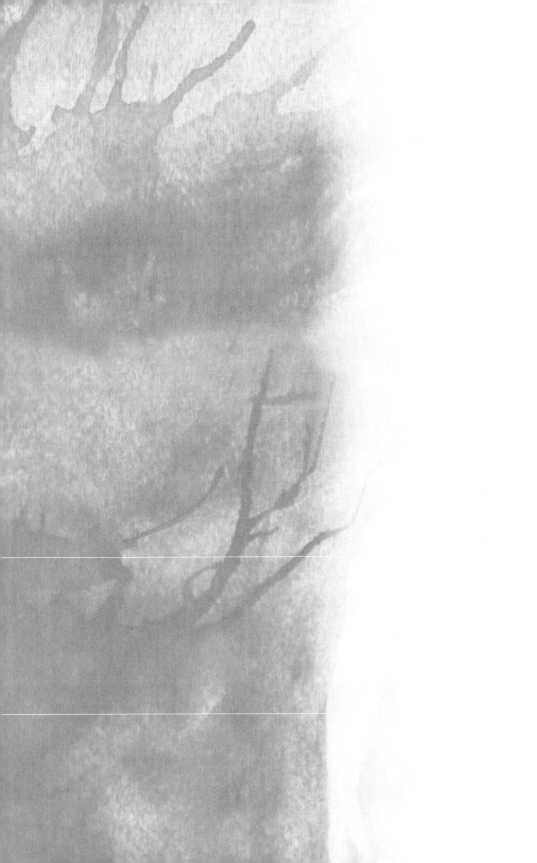

CHAPTER 16

OPEN Interactions

One of the benefits of being able to identify potentially risky behaviors is the opportunity to learn how to recognize those behaviors in your own interactions with children. All adults need to take the time to examine their own behaviors with children, looking to see whether there is anything inappropriate or compromising for either the child or the adult. Establishing personal standards for appropriate behavior will help adults become more aware of risky behaviors as well as preventing false accusations that can ruin reputations and interrupt lives.

In addition to the need to be aware of conditioning behavior as discussed in Chapter 7, other standards of behavior can help maintain a safe and supportive environment. For example, when interacting with children, adults should at least apply certain obvious principles and standards such as:

- Never possess or use illegal drugs or alcohol when working with children.

- Take care to protect all parties from health risks; that is, refrain from participating in activities when you are ill, and particularly when you are contagious.

- Use a team approach to managing activities whenever possible.

- Do not allow children to stay overnight alone with a single, unrelated adult in private accommodations.

- Do not make risqué comments or tell sexual jokes to or around children.

- Do not touch children in a provocative or suggestive way.

- Do not show children pornography or other adult material, and never involve them in pornographic, sexual, or provocative activities.

Most people will read these standards and wonder why it is necessary to state the obvious. But look around and see what's going on in the environment around you. Listen to the news and notice how little common sense is being demonstrated. It seems to be a rare commodity. When that is the case, it is sometimes necessary to state the obvious.

In addition to dealing with these obviously inappropriate situations, there are other circumstances that demand attention and rarely get it. For example, there is the very real dilemma of dealing with those who, because they have no intention of wrongdoing, never think to assess their own behavior to see whether it appears to be inappropriate. Those who only have an interest in wholesome, healthy interactions with children rarely think to establish standards of behavior. They think their behavior is fine because their intentions are proper.

Included in this equation are emergency situations nobody thought to prepare for. People think about obvious potential dangers such as rides or activities that are risky in nature. Children and adults are required to wear life jackets on boats, for example, and helmets are part of the bicycling equipment. However, people rarely evaluate seemingly harmless activities by looking to see what could go wrong and then doing whatever it takes to be prepared to deal with challenges. In this regard, we could all take a lesson from Scouting and "be prepared." This may add preparation time to activities and events but it will be time well spent, particularly if an emergency arises. For instance, how will you deal with an outsider who appears at an event with a camera and proceeds to take pictures of random children without permission from anyone at the event?

Both being prepared for emergencies and critically reviewing one's own behavior to avoid creating compromising situations are important in the effort to create and maintain safe environments. Applying an appropriate standard to all our interactions with children can make the difference in whether children, and the adults who interact with them, are at further risk of harm. However, it is not practical to assume that everyone who works or interacts regularly with children will start to consider all of their interactions by applying a uniform set of standards until and unless there is an easy way to remember the key elements, and a simple way to apply the principles at a moment's notice.

In order to create a set of standards that are easy to remember and easy to apply, we have created an easy-to-remember acronym that points to the key elements of appropriate interactions with children. Make sure all interactions with children are *OPEN*; that is, they are Observable, Proper, Effortless, and Non-sexual.

Observable

Interactions between adults and children other than their own kids should be visible, public, and available for all to see. One of the behavioral warning signs of a potentially risky adult is when someone manages to structure time with the child in a way that secludes the adult and child. Adults who pose a real risk to children want to make sure no one can see them interacting with the child. They want to have time and privacy to groom the child without the interference of others who might try to intervene in their plans.

Responsible adults make sure their activities with children are visible to others. They use public venues for their work with children and schedule their time together when they know others will be around. They let others know when they are meeting alone with children in a tutoring session or coaching environment, for example, and they let people know it is okay to drop by and check in during that time. Their work and play with children is open for all to see.

Making sure that these times with children are observable is a responsible and easy way to allay any concerns about the relationship between adults and children they are not related to. In addition, it is important for those relationships to be open and observable in families. Everyone wants some private time with their mom or dad but leave the door open during those times and make sure everyone is comfortable. If the child wants some private time, make time to do that, but let others know about it and make sure they know the child requested it.

The key is "observable." Child molesters are secretive and work hard to seclude children in areas where they can seduce the child without being seen or interrupted. Taking time and making the effort to assure that interactions between children and adults are visible, or at least available for others to see, can eliminate any concern about the intentions of the adult involved.

Proper

Adults must learn to think through their interactions with children to be sure the activities are appropriate. In this regard, there are a number of things to consider. First, as we all know, children want what they want, when they want it. Giving in to their desires and whims without approval from parents is risky and inappropriate. When children ask, or even beg, for something that parents would not agree with, you must say "no" until you clear it with the responsible adult. In rare instances, there may be an exception that arises because of emergency health or safety issues, but third-party adults must honor the wishes and the rules set down by parents and guardians, even when they think they know better or when they know the child wants something different.

Another area to consider is the need to follow the rules as they relate to the organization. Know the policies and procedures that apply to the interactions and follow them carefully. Let the wisdom of the team who created guidelines be the arbiter of any concerns, confusion, or unlikely situation.

Proper actions require that you take stock of the way you interact with children to make sure nothing you are doing is acting as a conditioning agent. For example, take a careful look at your physical contacts with children. Is there anything you are doing or any way you are touching them that could either

- condition the child to be willing to accept touch that is more intimate than is appropriate, or

- condition the community to accept certain public contact that is not as it should be?

Paying attention to the propriety of interactions simply means to think before you act. Consider, before you touch a child who is not your own, whether the interaction would be completely safe and wholesome through the eyes of another.

Be alert to the time and place of interactions with children. Make sure meetings are in proper, public locations, and the timing assures that others will be around. Remember that risky adults schedule time with children in secluded places at times that assure they are not observed. Make a practice of openness in your meetings with children and there will be no question about propriety.

Finally, be attentive to the nature and frequency of physically touching other people's children. Be thoughtful about where you touch a child. Look for ways that do not raise concerns. There are many appropriate forms of showing affection towards children other than your own. Among the most familiar are:

- Hugs standing side by side or with arms around shoulders.

- Pats on the shoulder or back.

- Hand-shakes.

- "High-fives" and hand slapping.

- Verbal praise.

- Touching hands, faces, shoulders, and arms.

- Holding hands walking with small children.

- Pats on the head when culturally appropriate. (For example, this gesture typically should be avoided in some Asian communities).

- Hugging shoulder-to-shoulder or hugging by touching faces cheek-to-cheek.

These physical contacts between adults and children are entirely proper. They are visible manifestations of the adult's responsibility for leaving everyone in the environment with the right impression and causing no one concern.

Effortless

Interactions between adults and the unrelated children in their environments should be easy and comfortable. For adults, one of the most effective ways to assure interactions meet this standard is to leave it up to the child. This means, for example, unless there is a safety issue involved such as a busy street, letting the young person initiate hand-holding or hugging.

Leave it to the child to initiate contact of any kind. A child in need of a hug will reach out, and as long as you make sure the care you give is public and non-sexual, no one will be concerned.

Only in an emergency should the adult force physical contact with the child or young person. If a car is coming and the child is in the way, the only thing that matters is safety.

The point is to leave casual or unintended contact to the child. Don't seek it out. Don't make the first move. Contact that is and appears to be effortless will be contact that is spontaneous and at the request of the child.

Non-sexual

One might say this goes without saying, but as we have seen many times, it is these simple, common-sense things that need reinforcing. Taking for granted that others will think of them or pay attention to them is fool's play.

Overtly sexual contact of any kind between children and adults — whether they are family or not — is inappropriate and must be eliminated. Adults also must take extra care to make sure there is no "accidental" sexual contact or that any accidental contact that is confusing or scary is explained quickly to the child along with an apology.

However, "non-sexual" does not just mean obviously sexual physical contact. There are other kinds of interactions that could be considered sexual or that have sexual undertones. Adults must learn to recognize these and make sure that they, too, are eliminated from the interactions they have with children.

Adults must be careful about lengthy embrace, or of inviting children over two years of age to sit on their laps. Pats of affection on the back or shoulder are appropriate, but adults should avoid touching children on the knees or legs.

Leave piggyback rides to dads and grandpas. The intimacy of this kind of contact is confusing to children and gives the wrong impression to others who see it.

One other area where awareness is important is in conversation and casual comments. Adults should be mindful of how they compliment children. Eliminate compliments that relate to physique or body development. Comments about a child "getting taller" or other references to growing up are fine and entirely appropriate, but avoid commenting in any manner that includes a sexual overtone. From time to time, you may have a comment about the inappropriateness of certain clothing or certain behavior. This is, in most cases, exactly what is expected of responsible adults working with children. However, comments such as those one might make to a date, a spouse, a close friend, or when trying to get a date, are not appropriate conversation material for talks with children.

As always, there is a caveat to this conversation. If your responsibility is to lead a conversation or discussion about provocative dress, make-up, or demeanor, then some of the conversation may include demonstrations of the types of comments these can generate. The point is to make sure that, as an adult working with children, your comments and compliments regarding their appearance and behavior are completely non-sexual and appropriate.

Taking on being *OPEN* in all of your interactions with children will assure those around you that your intentions are appropriate and wholesome. Being aware of these four simple areas for attention in your interactions with children will assure you the freedom to be with those around you, and will care appropriately for the children in your environment without placing yourself or them at risk or raising concerns for others.

Practice being *OPEN* in all your interactions with children. All that is required is a little attention to your own behavior and that of the children around you. The result will be a more open, free, and caring relationship for all those involved, and a care-free atmosphere where children and adults can thrive.

CHAPTER 17

Organizational Responsibility

When individuals take responsibility for being *OPEN* in their relationships with children, the possibility of creating and maintaining safe environments for children is greatly enhanced. When that effort is coupled with responsible action on the part of the organizations that provide programs and services to children, the possibility of interrupting the grooming process and protecting children from sexual predators is dramatically expanded.

Organizations today cannot ignore the responsibility of screening applications for staff and volunteer positions in programs for children or establishing structures and guidelines that support safe environments. Various entities have made worthwhile efforts to create standards for screening and selection processes that are available to assist organizations in getting this accomplished. Included in the appendix of this book are several tools for reviewing and monitoring the areas of organizational responsibility that are addressed in this Chapter. These tools are the result of years of examination and review of labor and employment law, as well as the thoughtful development of screening and selection tools and other structures for creating safer work and play environments for all concerned. In addition to forms and guidelines, the tools include a checklist for organizational responsibility in this area, and an assessment tool the organization can use to create the safest environment possible for the children and adults who work and play there.

Knowing there are structures and processes that can make a difference in the commitment to safety and support for everyone is step one. However, without a thoughtful consideration of the reasons for having these tools and a careful construction of the pieces used in your organization, the tools will become pieces of paper in a file or notebook, or worthless, time-consuming processes that make no real difference in the quality of life for all those who participate. Knowing and understanding why these processes and structures are important to the safety of children and adults is essential to an effective program that empowers adults and protects children.

Creating a safe and nurturing environment begins with applying scrutiny to those who want to participate with children.

Screening and background checks

Just because someone wants to work with children and appears to have the time and the ability to relate well to them does not mean they are *entitled* to work with children or that giving them the position is in the best interest of the children, the organization, or the volunteer.

Allowing someone access to children because of their apparent good intentions or their willingness to take on tasks no one else wants to do is careless and irresponsible.

Those who are granted the privilege of working with our children must be the ones who truly deserve the responsibility and the opportunity. This means everyone who wants to work with children must go through a screening process that includes a thorough background check.

A screening process is more than a cursory review of a few items on a checklist or a look to see if someone has a criminal history. The process must begin with laying the groundwork for what you expect to accomplish in the screening process and how to use the information gathered. Create criteria for all positions that interact with children, and then look to see what screening guidelines will give you information as to the fitness of an individual to provide what is wanted and needed for the position and the situation. Identify any areas of particular concern that deserve attention. In other words, know who you are looking for based on character, skills, and experience. Then find out whether candidates fill the bill.

Write job descriptions for each position that will be filled by staff or volunteers. Be prepared to explain the job and the physical requirements of the position to each applicant. Also, decide in advance who should be involved in the hiring or selection process for each position and make sure everyone is looking for the same qualities and using the same criteria.

Before you begin, consult an attorney to make sure the processes, job descriptions, applications, etc. are consistent with Title VII of the Civil Rights Act or any other federal or state laws that may apply to the organization regarding discrimination in hiring, selection, or organizational responsibility for the actions of volunteers and staff. A legal opinion is essential, and operating as if you are just getting some volunteers and don't really need to be this rigorous about the process is asking for trouble. Do it right as part of your commitment to create and sustain safe environments — not just to avoid liability. Protecting children from predators is the real reason for taking these steps.

Background checks are an essential part of the process but they are not just about criminal histories. They have a two-fold purpose. Criminal background must be checked to make sure none of the applicants seeking access to our children is a known predator or has a criminal history that points to a possible risk to children. The most effective criminal background checks include every state where the applicant has lived, using fingerprints as the basis of the search.

There are a number of reputable companies that can conduct reliable searches. However, criminal background checks are not enough. Criminal background checks only provide information on those who were reported, charged, and convicted of a crime that raises red flags for you or resulted in their appearance on a sex offender registry. Assuming the research is correct and most child molesters are not ever reported. (Bagley, 1992; Courtois & Watts, 1982; Finkelhor & Browne, 1986; Swanson & Biaggio, 1985) most risky adults will have no criminal background to discover. This does not mean we can ignore this part of the process; it just means that we can't expect too much from it. It will only tell us what it can tell us.

On the other hand, remember that child molesters really believe they live outside the rules that apply to the rest of us. (See Chapter 9) As a result, a predator may fill out an authorization for a criminal background check thinking that nothing will really come of it. In the predator's mind, there is the possibility that the organization will decide not to actually process the criminal review. Perhaps the organization will decide that the very fact the applicant is willing to submit to a background check is enough to assure it there is nothing to find. After all, no one in their right mind would sign an authorization knowing that they appear on a registry — or would they?

Or maybe the organization will conduct random checks due to the cost of processing everyone. Predators will think of these possibilities, and then evaluate the organization and people in charge to decide whether it is worth the risk to simply sign the waver and hope for the best. It is this type of thinking that protects predators from discovery when a simple check of sex offender registries would turn up the information needed to stop the person from gaining access to children.

Remember that predators are not in their "right mind" and relating to them as if they are is risky business and a waste of time. No organization can afford to let down its guard in this respect. Take every opportunity to find new ways to scrutinize those who want to work with children.

Be aware that in addition to the criminal background check, there are several other aspects to a comprehensive screening process. Among those are the completion of an application by candidates for both staff and volunteer positions, and checking references for everyone who applies. The application should include the applicant's history of work with children as well as a list of personal and work references.

Although some elements of the applications for staff and volunteers are similar, there are distinct differences that apply to each of them. For example, well-written staff applications include questions and statements such as:

- The consequences of falsifying information.

- A statement of the at-will employment policy of the organization.

- Requests for reference checks from previous employers.

- Notice about required alcohol or drug-testing (this testing should only be conducted after an offer of employment).

- A notice of the organization's policy about retaining applications and resumes.

There are also things that should NOT be part of an employment application. For example:

- No questions about HIV or AIDS testing.

- No questions about marital status, divorce, mental, or physical health.

- No questions about how long someone has lived at their current residence or whether the person is a homeowner.

- No questions about height or weight or any questions that, if answered, could provide information about a person's religion, ethnicity, age, disability, race, or gender.

Applications for employment must be constructed carefully to avoid potential liability issues. Applications for volunteers should follow the same principles and guidelines. The only exceptions are that volunteers are not staff so there is no need for a volunteer application to include a statement of "at-will" employment and volunteer applications should ask for the person's history of working with children. Employment history may or may not be relevant, depending on the kind of work the volunteer applicant has done, but a record of work with children is essential.

Regardless of whether the position is for staff or volunteers, organizations must take the time to call references. Talking with former employers or supervisors is the only way to really find out, as best you can, whether the applicant is someone who can be trusted working with children.

When calling references for volunteers, there are some additional questions one might ask to acquire the necessary information. For example, ask whether any adults or children ever complained about the person or had concerns about anything the applicant was doing in the program. Find out whether there were ever any decisions made to limit the person's contact with children or any actions taken to revise their volunteer assignments because of inappropriate or suspicious situations.

It is imperative that the references relied on to accept a volunteer or staff person be able to talk about the applicant's interactions with children. If the references provided cannot answer questions about this, the organization must go back to the applicant for other names or other contacts.

In addition, personal interviews with applicants are critical to the screening process. During these meetings, applicants and interviewers get to know something about one another, and the meeting is an opportunity to make organizational policies and procedures clear. Applicants need to know what is expected of them and they need to know that Codes of Conduct and policies and procedures are strictly enforced.

The personal interview is also a great place to explore the thoughts, ideas, and interests of the applicant that are evident in responsibilities of the available position. For example, ask open-ended questions that encourage applicants to explain more about their own background, interests, and experience. Ask things like:

- What kind of management or supervisory style do you prefer from those you work for?

- Would any of your references say they would not recommend you working with kids? If so, why?

- Why do you want this position?

- What is it about working with children that interests you?

- What do you think are the most important qualities we should look for in applicants for this position?

Also, pay attention to the job description for the available position. People who will be operating with a great deal of independence or who will work mostly one-on-one with children must have more stringent scrutiny. This doesn't mean, however, that it is okay to relax the screening process for people with no regular one-on-one-contact. Everyone who has contact with children must go through a rigorous screening process. When the person seeks to fill a position that is, by its nature, a more vulnerable situation for everyone involved, take the rigor up a notch.

All of these elements are essential to a screening process that offers the best opportunity for creating a safe environment for the children who come to and through your organization.

Remember that no one is entitled to access to children just because they are generously offering their time and talent to the children. The privilege of being entrusted with our most precious treasure, our children, goes only to those who deserve that trust.

Take the time to do the proper screening of anyone who wants to work with children. It will be worth the effort in the long run. Overlooking any pieces of the process can be costly for everyone if a predator sneaks into your organization and uses his or her position to molest children.

The screening process can be costly both in terms of the human resources needed to complete the process and the time required to do a proper screening. Find creative ways to address the issues of time and expense when developing a plan for screening adults. For example, if your organization has a board of directors or a pool of volunteers, look to see whether there are people with human resources experience among them. Ask them to donate some time to help you screen and select applicants for positions that involve working with children. If there is no one in your organization who can do this for you, contact your local RSVP[1] organization or SCORE[2] and ask for one or more senior volunteers who can work with you to get this process in place and completed.

Look for opportunities to use all the resources available to you to accomplish the goals of screening and selecting the right volunteers for your organization and the children you serve. The children, their parents, and those who already volunteer and work in the organization's programs and projects are counting on the organization's diligence.

The screening process is just the beginning. When your staff and volunteers are ready to go to work, you need to provide them with guidelines for acceptable interactions between children and adults. In the next Chapter, we explore how to establish, publish, and enforce boundaries the organization believes are appropriate between adults and the children they serve.

---

1 *Retired Senior Volunteer Program*, a program of Senior Corps, http://www.seniorcorps.org/

2 *Service Corps of Retired Executives*, a non-profit organization that provides expert assistance to small businesses nationwide. http://www.score.org/index.html

CHAPTER 18

Code of Conduct

One might think that applying common sense to potentially risky situations would address most of the risks involved. However, when we take a cold hard look at the world around us we can see that there is a decided lack of common sense evident in society today. Therefore, it is important that organizations set boundaries for employees and volunteers, particularly in their interactions with children.

Establishing a Code of Conduct for volunteers, staff, and program participants is an excellent way to accomplish four important goals.

- First, everyone participating gets clear about the standards of behavior that are expected from everyone in the program, regardless of their position.

- Second, the standards of behavior established in the Code of Conduct provide clarity for everyone. There is no confusion about what is and is not acceptable behavior.

- Third, volunteers, staff, and participants all know that the organization is committed to a safe environment for children and the adults who work with and care for them. By adopting and enforcing policies that identify what's appropriate and what's not between adults and the children in the program, the organization is asserting its commitment to the well-being of everyone involved.

- Fourth, everyone involved can turn their attention to positive actions and interactions that serve the real objectives and mission of the program and activities.

Creating a Code of Conduct can be a challenging task. Ideally, the document would give everyone a road map to appropriate interactions under all circumstances. However, that is unrealistic, so the important thing is to make sure certain areas are covered, and the principles applied in developing the Code of Conduct are clear and could be applied to any situation that arises.

One of the first considerations to address when creating a Code of Conduct is enforcement. How will compliance with the Code be monitored and enforced? These are sometimes difficult questions to answer but without a clear plan for monitoring and enforcement, a Code of Conduct will have virtually no value to anyone. A document that sits on the shelf or rests quietly in a nice binder will do nothing to protect children or the adults who spend time with them.

There are many good examples of enforcement practices in the human resources literature. In addition, progressive discipline structures can easily be adjusted to apply to volunteers as well as staff. This type of procedure assures people they are part of a process that does not overreact, but acts responsibly when something is amiss. However, don't assume that monitoring and enforcement are the same thing. Enforcement and monitoring are different and both are essential to the protection of all concerned. This is how we know what is happening in programs, activities, and classrooms. When creating the Codes of Conduct and enforcement and monitoring processes, ask questions like:

- How will we know the Code of Conduct is being followed?

- How will we monitor activities in remote or secluded parts of the facility?

- How will we know what's happening when volunteers or staff meet one-on-one with children?

- How can we monitor randomly?

- How should the monitoring process differ for those who work in teams with groups of children and those who work more closely in one-on-one situations?

- How do we monitor offsite activities?

- How can we teach everyone the importance of monitoring ourselves and each other?

Answering these questions will help the organization set up a process for monitoring adults who work with children.

There are some important elements to pay attention to when creating the Code of Conduct. For example, acknowledging situations that pose a greater risk of harmful or inappropriate behavior can assure that the thoughtfulness and creativity of those developing the Code is applied to these high risk situations. For example, it is harder to monitor behavior in secluded parts of a camp or on an overnight trip to a sponsored event. Thinking about these things in advance and creating a plan for making sure the Code of Conduct is the guiding principle for all activities can go a long way toward making sure the event or activity is fun for everyone.

In addition to monitoring and enforcement, the organization must decide on appropriate consequences for failure to comply with the Code of Conduct. As a practical matter, it may be difficult to come to an agreement about consequences until the Code is written and the standards are established.

When developing the Code of Conduct, many things must be included. However, it is important to start by establishing principles that guide the development of the Code of Conduct. For example, some organizations such as the Boy Scouts can establish a "two-deep leadership" principle that prohibits one-on-one interactions. In that paradigm, there must *always* be two adults present when children are around. This standard will work for some organizations, but not all. Therefore, when considering this principle as an essential part of the Code, it may be necessary to modify your approach to accommodate the practicalities of the environment in which your programs and services are provided. Although, in principle your organization may agree with this concept, a modification may be necessary to make it work for you. Among the alternatives that may be considered are:

- Applying the two-adults-present policy in high risk situations such as overnight activities, trips taken in private cars, camping, or other outdoor activities.

- Including extra supervision, additional training, in-depth screening, or other precautions when the mission of your organization is such that one-on-one contact is necessary. (i.e. mentoring, tutoring, counseling programs, etc.)

- Setting standards for the number of adults required in any given situation based on the age or developmental level of the children, the nature and location of the activity, and the potential risk in the situation.

Remember that the goal of this part of the Code is to limit the amount of time and the occasions when adults and children will be isolated from others. As always, the goal is to create and sustain a safe environment for everyone involved.

Another guideline for creating the Code of Conduct is the value of being able to distinguish between appropriate, inappropriate, and harmful behaviors. Take time to set standards for these three types of behaviors and begin to apply the standards to typical interactions with children. Although most people think they would prefer a list of do's and don'ts, establishing guidelines is most effective in the long run.

There certainly will be some behaviors that the Code will expressly prohibit but there is no way every contingency can be considered. Give each adult working with children standards for appropriate, inappropriate, and harmful behaviors and provide some examples. In addition, consider creating a Volunteer Code of Conduct that addresses some of the more obvious do's and don'ts for volunteers. It seems silly to have to tell adults that they must not use illegal drugs or drink and drive when working with children, but just as with the dearth of common sense in society today, some things really do not "go without saying," even when they should. "Better say than sorry."

Finally, remember that the goal of the activities and the programs is to provide support and services to children in an environment that nurtures and supports them. No Code of Conduct should be so restrictive that it places undue barriers between children and the adults who interact with them.

At the end of the day, the organization must protect the children it serves and, at the same time, encourage positive interactions that leave children feeling valued and special. Children need the kind of caring connections that support their development. Be careful to ensure that the Code of Conduct does not become a barrier to communication or to being with children in a way that makes a difference.

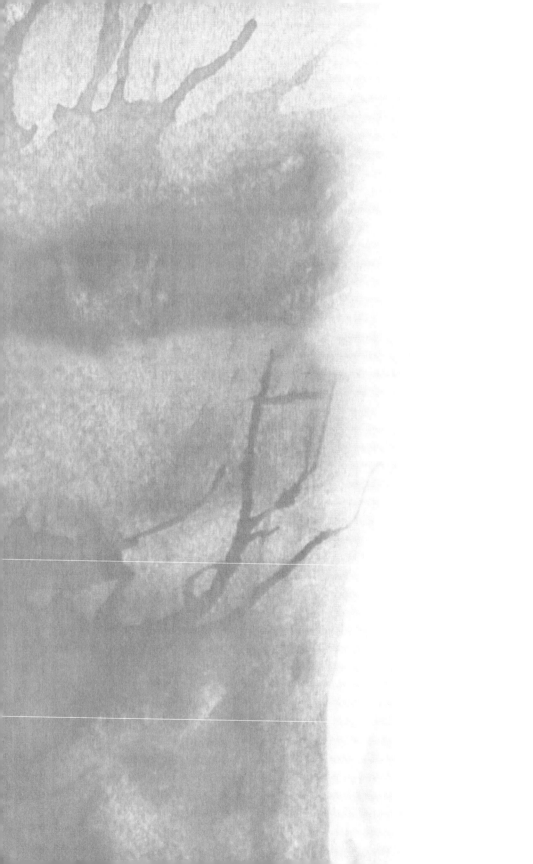

CHAPTER 19

Creating & Monitoring Access

In addition to paying attention to the people who are working and interacting with children, organizations must pay attention to the physical environment. Establishing policies and procedures as guidelines for creating safe environments is another important element for organizations. Some of these guidelines establish environmental protections such as locking doors to rooms that are not being used or trimming hedges so no one can use them for cover to grab someone. Others are designed to give direction to the community about how to preserve a safe environment.

Policies that create community guidelines need to be customized to your community. For example, if there are people who occasionally have keys to the facility, the organization should have written policies about how, when, or for what the keys may be used. If the organization sponsors events or field trips, policies should tell organizers how to manage the events including the standards for the ratio of adults to children, etc.

In addition to environmental and community guidelines, policies and procedures should include emergency situations. One of the most effective ways to create policies and procedures for dealing with emergencies is to gather key staff and volunteers and brainstorm about the kinds of situations that might arise. Create a list of possible scenarios, both from situations that have happened in the past and risks that volunteers and staff can anticipate.

When creating these policies, remember that no one can expect to anticipate every contingency or every possible emergency. However, a thoughtful look at the events and activities sponsored by the organization will give the team a good perspective of the kinds of emergency situations that are most likely to happen.

Once this list is developed, look it over to see if there are similarities or threads running through more than one scenario that could help the team identify actions which, if taken in advance, could prevent the emergency. After working through the similar situations, look to see what other policies or procedures could prevent emergencies or provide guidelines for dealing with them appropriately. Establishing and applying preventive procedures is obviously the best way to handle any emergency.

Sometimes, however, even our best efforts are not enough to prevent emergencies. Unexpected situations arise, accidents happen, people turn out to be unreliable. In those situations, the organization needs emergency procedures in place that call for actions or establish principles to protect children and adults. Even policies like the Boy Scouts' requirement that there be at least two leaders present at all times does not work in an emergency or if there is an accident. Teaching adults the principles that underlie the policies can help them make decisions in emergency situations requiring swift action. For example, if everyone knows the importance of communication, then, in an emergency, the adult faced with a situation that does not fit well into any policy would know to communicate what is happening to someone in a supervisory role immediately and work out a solution with that person or, at least let the other person know what is going on and how it is being handled.

No group could plan for every possible contingency but looking at the likely scenarios and establishing solid principles on which to rely is a great foundation for protecting both children and adults. In addition, the establishment of rules, policies, and procedures, and the organization's commitment to enforcing them, are essential parts of the goal of preventing child sexual abuse. Remember that one of the warning signs that someone is a potential risk of harm to children is a disregard for the rules — any and all rules. If everyone in the organization is expected to follow the policies and procedures and obey the rules, the one who refuses to do so or who thinks the rules just don't apply to him or her becomes noticeable. It should be like a big red flag is painted on the person's forehead saying, "Watch me!"

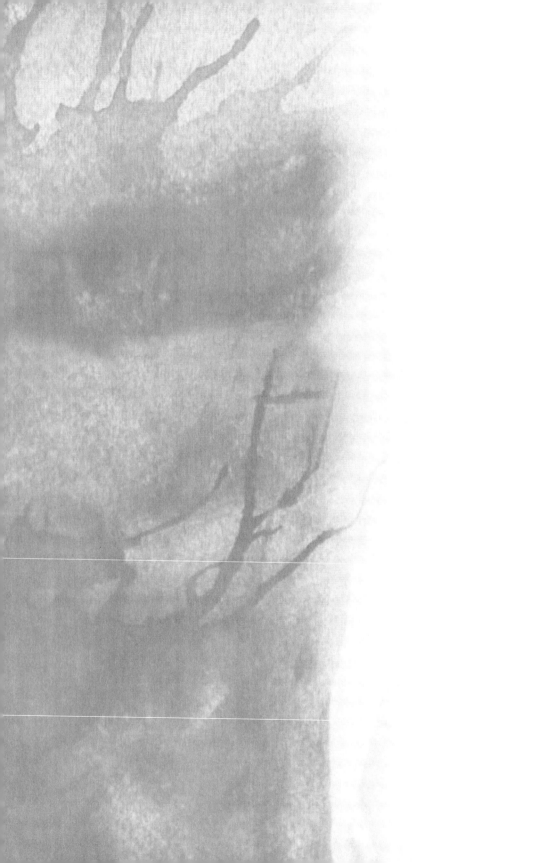

CHAPTER 20

Monitor the Environment

Safe environments are not created just by establishing attitudes and actions that promote safety. Another aspect is the need for safety in the physical environment. Polices about locking doors to rooms that are not being used are easier to follow if unused offices and classrooms are simply refitted with new locks that don't open with old keys.

There is a great way to check out the safety of the environment and, at the same time, educate adults about the elements that create risk and what it takes to make things safe. Take a walk through the environment with others who work or volunteer there.

Gather a group of adults or teens who work or volunteer in a particular building or space. Divide them into teams of at least three people and send them out to look over the facility and note any challenging or dangerous situations. Make a list of the kinds of things to look for that need attention. For example:

- Places where there is no lighting.

- Places where equipment is stored in a way that creates a secluded spot.

- Any location where there are cracks in sidewalks or problem areas in walkways or hard surfaces.

- Areas that are "off the beaten path" and, as a result, are unsecure.

- Security systems that don't work or have codes that are common knowledge.

- Any kind of physical hazard that has gone unnoticed.
- Landscaping that creates hazards, such as bushes that are large and planted far enough away from the building that there is room for someone to hide and not be seen.

Finding these threats to physical safety can make a world of difference for everyone. Not only does correcting these situations enhance personal safety, but calling attention to unsafe areas reminds everyone of the need to pay attention and to correct problems that arise.

There can also be unexpected benefits from these actions. For example, one church in the Midwestern part of America did a walk-through looking for places that might present risks to children and noticed that a curb area by the parking lot was very dark at night. With a number of senior citizens attending regularly, winter evening services were clearly presenting a serious safety risk that had gone unnoticed. Motion-sensitive lights were installed in the area to light the way when it was dark.

The interesting side benefit is that the church was in an area bordering an economically-depressed part of the city that had become a breeding ground for gang activity. The church parking lot had become a gathering place for a large gang. When members of the gang would gather, the pastor, who lived on the property, would call 911 and report the gathering. By the time police arrived, the gang would be out of sight until the police left, and then they would reappear. With the installation of the motion- sensitive lights in the dark areas of the parking lot, the gang left on its own.

Monitoring the environment is an ongoing process. Quarterly or semi-annual walk-throughs can keep the organization's focus on the need for safety in the physical environment. It is an easy step but one that easily can be forgotten or overlooked.

CHAPTER 21

Using the Sex Offender Registry

What is a "Sex Offender Registry" and how can it help us protect children? In 1994, the Jacob Wetterling Act[3] made it mandatory that states create a list, or "registry," of people convicted of sexual crimes against children. Even before the mandate, however, California required sex offenders to register with the California Department of Justice Sex Offender Tracking Program. The program was established in 1947 and was the first in the nation. The requirements for registry in the California program remained consistent until 1986 revisions added new registration requirements to the law.

Many states include a broad range of sex offenses in the registry. Others list only those people convicted of a crime on a more limited list of offenses. For example, some states may limit those on the registry to persons convicted of sex crimes involving children. Others list all those convicted of major sex offenses regardless of the age of the victim. A website hosted by the US Department of Justice provides access to state sites.[4] There is no national registry yet, but progress is being made.

In 1996, the Jacob Wetterling Act was amended by adding what is commonly referred to as "Megan's Law."[5] This amendment gave states permission to make the lists available to the public. The Adam Walsh Child Protection and

---

3 42 USCA § 14071

4 www.nsopr.gov/

5 42 U.S.C.A. § 13701

Safety Act of 2006, P.L. 109-248, began to establish national standards for sex offender registries, and establishing those guidelines is in process.[6] When the legislation named for young Adam Walsh is fully implemented, there will be uniform standards for sex offender registries nationwide, and the expectation is that sex offenders will be much less able to slip through the cracks of the system by moving from state to state.[7]

Even before the Adam Walsh Act, the following crimes appeared on virtually every list:

- Sodomy

- Non-parental kidnapping

- Child molestation

- Incest

- Child pornography crimes (production, possession, and distribution)

- Sexual abuse of a minor

- Sexual battery of a minor

In addition, conviction of an attempt to commit any of these crimes warrants an appearance on the registry. In some states, listing on the registry is for life. Others, like Oklahoma, have a tiered system that rates the crime and the offenders, and determines the level of threat posed by each offender. Those who are a lower risk to the population are on the list for fewer years, and those who are a high risk are on the list for life. Regardless of the perceived risk over time, everyone goes on the list.

Sex offenders must register upon release from prison and are required to update their information each time they

_____

6 www.ojp.usdoj.gov/smart/pdfs/proposed_sornaguidelines.
   pdf

7 http://www.missingkids.com/

move. A sex offender who fails to register or gives false information is subject to further criminal charges. According to the Center for Missing and Exploited Children, there are already more than half a million *registered sex offenders* living in the United States. The public can locate the most currently available information about the individuals who might be living in their neighborhood through the Internet.

Having said all that, sex offender registries cannot protect children. They can inform parents and others about the location of convicted sex offenders who abide by the law, register, and give accurate information to authorities. That information is valuable to parents and other caregivers. Keeping children out of harm's way is one of the responsibilities of parents, guardians, and care givers in the effort to protect children.

There is a problem with sex offender registries, however. The problem arises when parents start relying on the registry to tell them where sexual predators are in their neighborhood and then think that knowing where the registered sex offenders are protects their children from being assaulted.

This raises several concerns in the commitment to prevent the sexual abuse of children. First, the registry can only tell you about child molesters who were reported, caught, charged, and convicted of a crime that resulted in them being listed on the registry. Most sex offenders are never reported, never caught, and never convicted of child molestation. So, they would never show up on the registry of any state.

Second, at this point, the registry search is only state-by-state, and if a predator moves across state lines and does not register in the new state, he or she usually goes undetected. It is possible for law enforcement to discover the failure to register if a convicted sex offender is arrested or questioned by law enforcement for any reason and criminal history is checked. If a sex offense is listed, law enforcement my look further to determine whether the offender is listed on the registry.

Third, keeping the information on the registry current is a challenge most states cannot seem to meet. Catching criminals that threaten public safety and welfare and dealing with present day crimes is, and should be, law enforcement's priority. Often, updating the system takes a back seat to current demands on staff time.

Fourth, some states do not include information about sex offenders who were convicted before public notification became the law. Those already in jail, and others who had served their sentences may not be listed regardless of the level of risk they present to the children in the community.

Perhaps most important is to remember most sex offenders are never reported, charged, and convicted, so they are not likely to be listed on a registry anywhere. Even those who are reported and charged may be able to bargain successfully with the state for conviction on a lesser offense and avoid being listed on the registry.

Even with their obvious limitations, registries are valuable. Regularly searching the registry is beneficial for adults committed to creating safe environments for all children. Adults need to make use of every tool available in order to protect children from sexual predators, and the Sex Offender Registry is one of those tools.

It is a benefit to know who is living in your neighborhood that poses a risk to children. Convicted sex offenders have a high rate of recidivism, and according to the Department of Justice, 60 percent of convicted sex offenders are on parole or probation at any given time. This means they are living in our neighborhoods, shopping in the stores we frequent, and participating with us in community activities and events.

When compared to non-sex offenders released from prison, the Department of Justice also says that sex offenders returning to society are four times more likely to be rearrested for a sex crime. Checking the registry provides conscientious adults valuable information for identifying convicted offenders in the neighborhood and keeping children away from them.

The registry also helps organizations screen applicants for jobs or volunteer positions. Checking the registry as part of the screening process is an important piece of a comprehensive effort to create safe environments and keep children safe as they participate in community, church, and neighborhood programs and services.

State and national resources are available on the Internet at places such as http://www.nsopr.gov, sponsored by the Department of Justice, and www.familywatchdog.us, one of several independent websites. Many states also have sites for their own registries.

Use the registry well. Regularly check your neighborhood, your community, and the people your children come in contact with. Checking people out is a responsible thing to do. It is not paranoid or disrespectful to look someone up on the registry. It is, however, important to remember to check out everyone, not just the people we think "look" like risky individuals or people we already have concerns about.

Sometimes we think we know what a child molester looks like or what group of people they might belong to. Those are myths and preconceived notions that can undermine our prevention efforts. Myths and preconceived notions about child molesters divert our attention from the only real opportunity we have to identify a potential child molester — identifying the behavioral warning signs of potentially risky adults.

The Sex Offender Registry is one more opportunity to be proactive in our commitment to protect children. Just don't rely on it as "The Answer" to whether someone is a risk of harm to children.

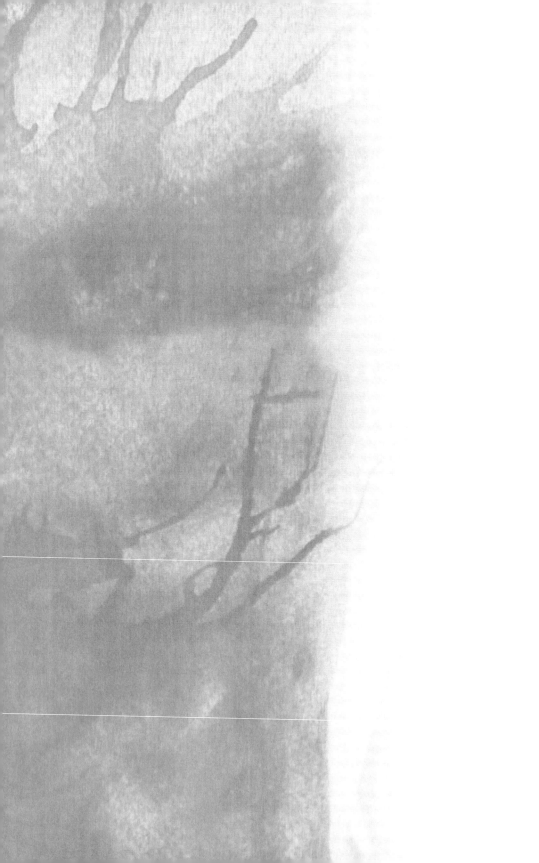

CHAPTER 22

Communicate and Act

Perhaps you've heard the saying, "Knowing makes no difference." What is really meant is that having knowledge is essential, but it is not enough. Two other things are necessary before any difference is made — communication and action.

By way of illustration, ask yourself whether you consider yourself to be even a little bit overweight. If the answer is "yes," ask yourself whether you know how to lose weight. If the answer again is "yes," and yet you are not doing what you know to do to be healthy and fit, you can begin to see that knowledge without action makes no difference. However, if you are actively working on your health and fitness, the knowledge you acquired about how to lose weight is essential to your success.

Applying the knowledge, practicing what you learned, being flexible, questioning, paying attention, and operating with careful analysis are important elements in being successful at any objective. These are the things we do to develop proficiencies in our life. To become proficient at recognizing potentially risky adults in the environment and intervening before a child is molested, we must bring the same elements and activities to this task.

We have information about the potentially risky behaviors of adults in our environment. Gathering all the information we can about those behaviors, and continuing to educate ourselves and train ourselves to be observant are the beginnings of accomplishing our goal. Recognizing those behaviors and taking action to intervene in risky or potentially risky situations is one way to prevent abuse.

Sometimes even intervention that interrupts a situation or a grooming process is not enough to protect our children. Sometimes we must take action to bring the concern to the attention of the adult in question, a supervisor, or, if we suspect that a child is being or has been abused, the authorities.

The problem is that one of the most difficult and challenging things for adults to do is to raise concerns about behavior with another adult, particularly a friend, a family member, or a colleague. When we take the time to think about it, we readily admit that if our behavior was causing anyone concerns about our interactions with children, we would want to know. In addition, we would prefer that concerns be communicated to us directly and as quickly as possible. That is the only way we can change what we are doing to make sure no one has a concern about the time we spend with children.

The truth is that people do not tell us about their concerns and we don't tell them about ours. When asked why we avoid talking to the person directly, even though we know sharing concerns is what is needed, there are usually four or five standard reasons given for keeping quiet.

Among the most common are:

Fear of being wrong. Fear that expressing a concern will be interpreted as an accusation stops people from taking action. They think they need "proof" that the concern poses a real threat to children before they say anything.

Fear of retaliation. Adults are afraid that expressing a concern will result in retaliation against them, their children, or their family. They talk themselves out of speaking up because they are afraid of repercussions. This is particularly true if the person behaving badly has some control over the observer's child or children. Adults want to protect children from the retaliatory acts of angry or resentful adults.

Concern about "making waves." Adults routinely evaluate a concern to decide what they think the impact of disclosure will be. If the risk of a negative or strong reaction seems high, they justify not saying anything in honor of not making waves.

Disbelief that there could be anything really wrong. It is almost impossible for adults to imagine that someone they trust, someone they have allowed into their families and lives, could be a predator. Therefore, it becomes very, very difficult for them to believe that this person's behavior is truly inappropriate. They want to think the best because it is too painful to think the worst. Sometimes, without asking any more questions, they immediately make excuses for the friend/family member.

"It's not my job." It is common for adults to relate to challenging situations at work or in volunteer situations as if they are the responsibility of someone else. People withhold communication because they believe that speaking up is not up to them. That responsibility belongs to someone else — someone in a position of authority.

These are all valid reasons for keeping quiet about concerns. The problem is that these reasons don't stop us from talking to *others* about our concerns; they simply stop us from talking to the right person – the person who can impact the situation.

We rarely talk to the person whose behavior concerns us or to that person's supervisor. We do talk to others. We talk to friends, neighbors, spouses, co-workers, and anyone else we think might be interested.

We ask others for their opinions about what we observed. We want to know what they think and whether they would be concerned. We look for agreement that our opinions and concerns are valid.

The danger in taking this route is that these conversations are, by definition, gossip and might even be considered slander.[8]

Gossip is "rumor or talk of a personal, sensational, or intimate nature." Expressing unverified concerns that an adult is behaving with children in a sexually inappropriate way to someone other than the person or people involved is certainly "sensational rumor of an intimate nature."

Gossip can do irreparable harm to someone's reputation. Anyone who has been the target of gossip knows how long it takes to undo the damage resulting from thoughtless or spiteful stories designed to hurt another's reputation. It can take months and sometimes years to repair the damage done by gossip. In some cases, the damage is permanent. No apology or public retraction can restore a person's good name.

Gossiping about someone in a manner that leaves concerns with others about whether this person is a child molester is the kind of rumor that does irreparable harm. In fact, irresponsible conversation about your concerns that someone might be a child molester can actually cause all of the things you are trying to avoid by refusing to speak directly to the person or persons involved. The consequences of this type of gossip are far reaching and devastating. Although the damage can be difficult to measure in financial terms, the person who is the subject of the gossip may bring legal action against you for any losses suffered as a result of your gossip. The bigger cost is to the reputation and good name of the individual who is the subject of the gossip — damage that can be avoided by communicating concerns directly to the person or persons involved, even if the person gets upset.

---

8 Slander is a legal term referring to "words falsely spoken that damage the reputation of another." Dictionary.com. WordNet® 3.0. Princeton Univ. http://dictionary.reference.com/browse/slander (accessed: November 19, 2008).

It should come as no surprise when people get upset about concerns raised by their behavior. People with good intentions do not want any of their actions to raise concerns, and those with bad intentions do not want to be noticed. Regardless of the intentions of the adult involved, there will be upset about concerns. However, the one with no bad intentions is likely to simply get to work to correct the problem, while the real risk to children will have a different response. The predator who draws attention is more likely either to go away and avoid further scrutiny or respond with righteous indignation and bravado — and take no corrective action. In the end, if you stand by your concerns and hold the adult accountable for changing behavior, children will be safer regardless of the adult's reaction or original intention.

Finally, never forget that it is only the behavior of the specific adult in question that raised concerns. For the most part, we want to trust the people who are there to care for, teach, and support our children. It is only when someone's behavior crosses a line that "red flags" are raised and concerns are expressed.

How to have "hard" conversations

Once you understand the importance of communicating your concerns to the person whose behavior triggered your uneasiness or to that person's supervisor, the question that arises is, "What do I say?" Perhaps this is the core of the problem adults have with communicating their concerns about another adult's behavior. All the reasons we come up with may be a smokescreen for the fact that we have no idea how to carefully and thoughtfully communicate a serious concern about someone's behavior towards children in a way that creates minimal upset and maximum impact.

There are some simple rules to follow to help create a powerful, effective communication that raises awareness about the specific concerns and, at the same time, causes the least amount of upset.

First, think through what you want to communicate and what you want to accomplish in the interaction. When something seems "off" to us, we are often faced with a couple of challenges. We don't know exactly what to say and we don't know for sure how to say it without causing unnecessary upset.

Taking time to think through the process, including what you want to accomplish, can make the difference in the success or failure of the communication. There are some questions to answer for yourself before you address the concern with the other person.

- *What exactly did you see that caused concern?* Begin by clearly and carefully describing the actions that raised concerns. Be able to tell someone exactly what bothered you including the adult's actions in the particular circumstances. Comments like "Something seems off." Or "I don't know exactly what it is but something about that situation bothered me" are not useful in these types of situations.

- *Why did the behavior raise concerns?* A good way to begin the conversation is by telling the person why it is necessary to talk about this at all. You will only be able to do this with respect and care if you are sure about the actions and circumstances that raised red flags for you.

- *Why did you decide to raise the concern with this particular person?* Think carefully about the best way to present the concern. If you decide to take it directly to the person involved, take the time to explain why you chose that route rather than speaking to a supervisor. On the other hand, if you go to the supervisor first, be clear about your reasons for going that route.

- **What do you want to accomplish in the communication?** You can already assume anyone faced with a conversation that raises concerns about interactions they are having with children is going to react and, in some cases, react strongly. It will make a big difference in the outcome of the communication if you are clear about what you want to accomplish. Perhaps you want to give the person a chance to see for herself or himself that some activities place children and adults at risk so that they can change. Perhaps you want to raise awareness about the risks involved in assuming that our intentions are the determining factor in how something is perceived by others. Whatever you want the result to be, create it before the conversation and that intention will be the context for the entire communication. Under those circumstances, a thoughtful, positive resolution is more likely.

- **What is the right time to have the conversation?** In one sense, there is no right time to have a conversation with someone about his or her behavior that raises concerns about their interactions with children. However, when it is necessary to have this conversation, create or choose a time that is respectful of the serious nature of the issue. Find a time and place that allow for some privacy. You do not want the conversation overheard by others. Make sure the setting is one that promotes the ability to focus on the conversation. If you have concerns about interactions involving children and young people, don't put the conversation off any longer than absolutely necessary. The only way to accomplish all of these objectives may be to set up a meeting quickly in a place that is away from the children. Taking the time to be cognizant of these factors will also speak to the person about the real intention being to raise awareness about a concern rather than to make an accusation.

- **Are you willing to include yourself in the conversation by asking others to monitor you?** One way to demonstrate the commitment to eliminating risky behavior from all our interactions with children is to be proactive. Asking others, including the person whose behavior gives you concern, to let you know if you ever do anything that raises concerns points to the real commitment that is driving the communication. If you are not willing to invite others to keep an eye on your interactions with children, you might want to reconsider why you are having the conversation at all. If the goal is really to create a safer environment for all concerned and you are willing to address other people's shortcomings, you ought to be willing to submit to the same scrutiny.

- **How will you follow through after the conversation?** Whether you are raising concerns about a co-worker, volunteer, neighbor, or member of the family, you must consider how you will follow up to make sure the concern gets addressed. It is not enough just to express your concern. Once you tell the person or the supervisor about the behaviors that raised concerns, you must find out whether the concerns are dealt with effectively and quickly. First, be sure that the person to whom you are speaking understands the communication. One of the best quotes to remember is this anonymous statement:

"The greatest problem in communication is the illusion that it has been accomplished."

Clarify the issue by simply finding out what the person heard you say. Ask! Clear up any misconceptions or misunderstandings right away.

Confusion and unclarity need to be resolved early to avoid unnecessary upset and anger.

In addition to making sure the issues are clear, remember that communicating the concern is not the end of the situation; it is the beginning of the resolution. Before you have the conversation, think about how much time to give the person to correct the situation, and let him or her know you will be following up to make sure the situation is resolved.

Be clear about the kind of change in behavior you will expect as evidence of good intentions and then watch for those behaviors. If they fail to show up in a timely manner, bring up the concern again. If it still remains unresolved, be prepared to take the issue to the supervisor or the supervisor's supervisor if necessary.

Answering these questions is pivotal to having an effective conversation with someone who is behaving in a way that raises concerns. When you are clear about your intentions from beginning to end, you have the best chance of impacting the situation in a way that produces the least stress and upset for everyone involved.

Don't be afraid to start the process of communicating your concerns. As long as you answer these questions, you can ensure your message is clear and unmistakable and the goal of creating a safe environment will be achieved. Once you start the process, do not stop until it is resolved to your satisfaction. Promoting and advocating for an environment where concerns are raised and resolved quickly is a powerful demonstration of your commitment to safe environments and protecting children.

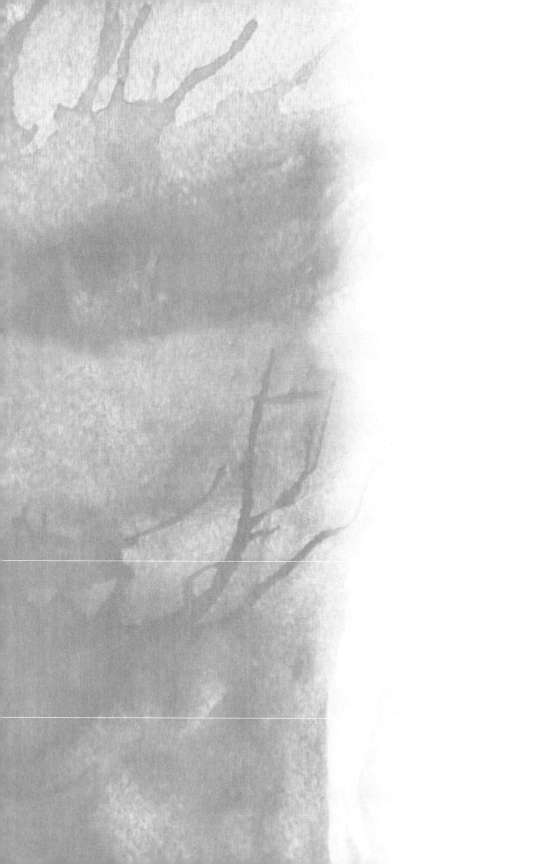

CHAPTER 23

Continuing to Learn

Over the years, our society has seemed to speed up considerably. Of course, the Internet is a major contributor to the demand for more, better, faster information, but over the years, we have become more and more impatient for results NOW! We want a pain pill that cures a major headache in 15 minutes. We want a patch that eliminates a 25-year smoking habit in two weeks. We want what we want immediately, and we want everything to work without much effort or patience.

The problem is that there is nothing easy or quick about stopping child sexual predators. To accomplish this goal requires more than a quick lesson in what to watch for. It requires practiced attention and patient observation that become more acute and proficient over time.

Television shows that "catch" predators have demonstrated that even nationwide humiliation on television will not stop a predator from pursuing his or her objectives. There is no cure for sexual predators – there is only prevention, and prevention demands that we be able to recognize the behaviors potential predators exhibit and intervene to stop them.

It is difficult to assimilate new ideas into our thinking and acting. In order to fully accomplish this goal, it is necessary to reinforce small bits of information over time until it becomes second nature to us. A really good way of thinking about the process is to remember how we learned our multiplication tables as young students. First, we were introduced to the idea of multiplication as a concept. We saw how it might make life simpler in the long run but the concept was foreign. It required us to think outside the box we had for math and begin to consider something besides addition and subtraction.

Once we started to examine the concept, our teachers presented us with a very real example of how it worked by having us confront "0" times anything. We started to see that no matter how many 0s there were in a row, the total would always be 0. Then we focused on 1s, and then the 2s, and we started to get a glimpse of the real value of multiplication. So we went to work memorizing the multiplication tables.

We did that work a little at a time. We practiced and repeated and practiced and repeated until we could multiply in our head almost without thinking. It took a long time, a lot of practice, and a great deal of intentionality to absorb the concepts and assimilate the answers into our thinking, but now, all these years later, we still multiply numbers in our head automatically. For example, if someone says that they need us to do something 3 times a week for the next 5 weeks, we have already done the math and know that means 15 times — even if the total number of times does not have any relevance to the conversation or the project. We still multiply because it is so automatic for us. We are proficient at multiplication. It has become second nature.

In order for us to become proficient at recognizing the risky behaviors of potential child molesters, we need to assimilate these behaviors into our thinking and our observations so that they, too, become second nature to us. To do that requires continuing practice and education.

Practice and continuing education are perhaps the most difficult parts of this process. We want to have the information. We want to stop predators. We want to protect our children and interrupt the grooming process, and we think knowing what to watch for should be enough to make that happen. The truth is, though, without lots of practice, we never become proficient at anything. Practice either occurs naturally as a matter of course because we are so focused on acquiring a skill, such as when we learned to drive, or it occurs because we regularly schedule occasions to turn our attention to the subject.

To become proficient at recognizing PRBs exhibited by any of the adults in the environment requires regularly scheduled occasions to reinforce the information. Only then can it become second nature to us. Like it or not, it takes work to become an expert at recognizing risky adult behaviors and interrupting them as part of our commitment to prevention.

Take time to join and gain access to the tools available through Empowering Adults – Protecting Children, Inc. at www.empoweringadults.org to continue to develop the skills necessary to prevent child sexual abuse. Spend some time each month focusing on one of the PRBs exhibited by potential child molesters and becoming proficient at recognizing inappropriate behaviors that could be an indicator that someone may be a child molester. Recognizing these PRBs and interrupting them is our best hope for protecting children from sexual predators. We must be as diligent about protecting children from predators as we are about other important things in life. Our children are counting on us.

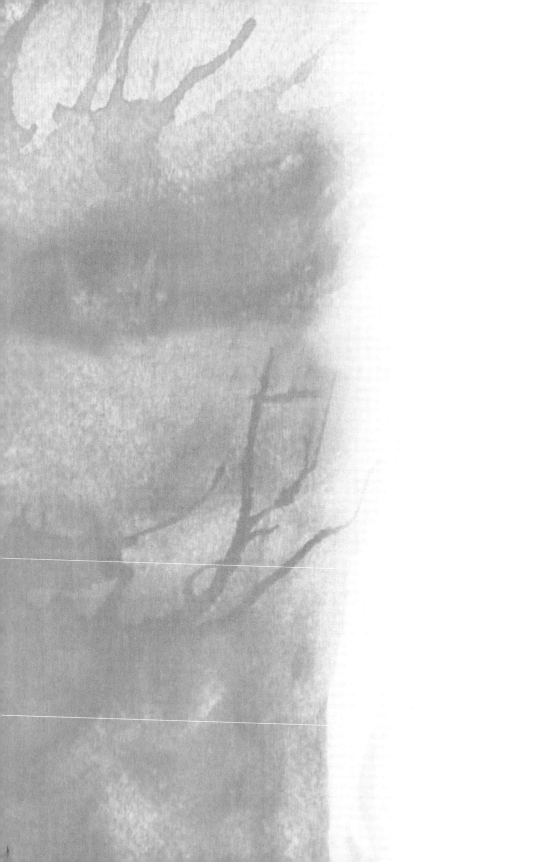

CHAPTER 24

Strengthening Children

If we learn how to recognize the risky behaviors exhibited by adults in our environment and take steps to interrupt those behaviors, we have begun to create an environment where child sexual abuse cannot occur.

To fully protect our children, we also need to supply them with tools to protect themselves. There are a number of things parents and guardians can do to empower children to be our partners in creating safe environments. The companion booklet to this book, *Keeping Them Safe*, provides parents with information they need to guide their children through to the safety tools that can help protect them from harm.

Among these tools are:

- *Teach children the touching rules.* As part of their personal safety education, children need to know the touching rules.

  No one is allowed to touch your private body parts (the parts of the body covered by a bathing suit) except to keep you clean and healthy. Very few people have permission to do that and only when your parents say it is okay and you are too little to do it yourself.

  If ANYONE, even someone you know and trust, touches you in a way that makes you feel uncomfortable, scared, or confused, you should:

  — Say "no" or words that sound like "no."

  — Get away as quickly as possible.

> *— Tell a trusted adult what happened —*
> *even if the person does not want you to tell*
> *anyone.*

It is up to the adults in children's lives to know these rules and to make sure children learn the rules. Parents and guardians need to teach the rules, and other responsible adults need to reinforce the rules and obey them.

- Teach children the proper names of their private body parts in the same way that they learn about the names of other body parts. Do not skip over the private parts. It sends a message to children that there is something different or bad about these parts or talking about these parts. Reluctance to be proactive with children in this area places them at risk. The American Academy of Pediatrics, experts at www.drspock.com, and other organizations committed to child safety and health, tell us that by the time children go to school, they should know the proper names of private parts, why those parts are private, the functions of the private parts, and the physical differences between girls and boys.

- Learn when it is developmentally appropriate to teach children about their private parts, the differences between girls and boys, how the private parts work, and the function of each. *Keeping Them Safe* includes tips on how to take advantage of teachable moments and how to present sometimes challenging information in a developmentally appropriate way.

- Find ideas and guidelines for setting safety rules for everyone in the family to follow. Tools assist families in creating rules that are proactive, teaching and empowering children to protect themselves. Children become partners with parents, guardians, and grandparents, and learn that they have some control in difficult and challenging situations. The same rules then become the guidelines and standards that parents and guardians can expect of other adults in the child's life. Parents learn to be clear about the rules and to take appropriate action with adults who regularly ignore or thumb their nose at the rules. They also learn how to establish rules for babysitters that are clear to the children and the sitter.

- In Chapter 15 we discussed the types of behaviors exhibited by Internet predators. *Keeping Them Safe* helps parents and guardians establish rules that can help keep children safe from these predators.

In addition to these tools for parents, guardians, and grandparents, *Keeping Them Safe* includes information about responding to disclosures from children. These are the most painful and difficult conversations adults have with children. We want to know what happened if our child is harmed; we just never want to have to hear that our child was abused in this way. A child's decision to disclose to a particular adult is a demonstration of tremendous faith and trust. Responding appropriately to the disclosure can go a long way toward reinforcing that trust and affirming that the child made the right decision.

There are three goals in any conversation that includes a disclosure of sexual abuse.

- First, to protect the child from further abuse.

- Second, to stop the perpetrators from abusing this or any other child.

- Third, to address the child's physical, emotional, and psychological needs; the harm done to the family; and, when appropriate, the community.

There are a number of factors that impact the long-term consequences of child sexual abuse. In addition to the type of sexual activity, the duration of the abuse, and level of trust broken by the adult perpetrator, a determining factor in recovery is the response of the adults and the community to the disclosure. The damage can be either intensified or diminished by the nature of the response to the disclosure. Children need to know that we can take it. They need to know that their disclosure is not going make things worse. For example, children are unlikely to disclose if they have heard parents, in response to news reports about sexual assaults of a child, say something like, "If someone did that to my child, I would blow his head off." They are afraid and they know that killing someone can mean the parent is arrested and taken away. The child will endure the abuse and keep quiet to make sure the parent is not put in a position of having to make good on that threat.

There are some important points to remember when a child discloses:

- *Do not panic or express shock* — No matter how upset you are, keep your attention on the needs of the child. Listen carefully and be open to hearing whatever the child has to say.

- *Find a private place to listen.* Listening to the child in private will demonstrate your respect for the child. **Do not question the child about what happened. Just listen to what the child has to say.** Only trained professionals should interview children. Questioning a child without the proper training and environment can compromise a formal investigation, and risk the safety and wellbeing of the child making the disclosures and any others that might be at risk.

- *Express your belief in the child* — Speaking up is scary. Children need support when they have the courage to speak up. Perpetrators threaten them with dire consequences if they tell anyone. When children overcome the fear and are willing to talk, we must trust them and accept their story as true. Always resolve any doubts you have in favor of the child.

Be particularly careful what you say in response to the disclosure. An offhand comment such as, "I cannot believe Uncle Joe would do that!" can be interpreted by the child as disbelief. When children think the adults in their life do not believe them about the abuse, they often recant and withdraw.

- *Let children know they are not at fault* — Children know that what the abuser did was wrong, but abusers blame the children so they often feel guilty about what happened. The children believe it was their fault and that they must have been a willing participant. Make sure the child understands that you know they are not at fault, you are there for them, and if there are any problems, they can come to you for assistance.

- *Assure the child that telling was the right thing to do.* — Children need a great deal of reassurance once they come forward to report abuse. The abuser has tried to convince the child that adults will not believe what the child has to say. It will take time to overcome the abuser's grooming tactics. Keep up the positive reinforcement.

- *Report the abuse and address the immediate needs of the child* [9] — Report the child's allegations and immediate needs to the proper authorities immediately. Make sure the child is protected and safe. Do not delay. Do not call parents first. Do not discuss it with others

---

9 Links to child protection services and the reporting laws in all 50 states may be found at www.empoweringadults.org. Click on "child abuse."

to decide whether to call. Do not wait for more information. Report!

Remember that your job is to listen and support the child – not to investigate the allegations.

- *Tell the child what will happen next.* — Be honest. Tell the child that you are calling the authorities and someone will be investigating. Do not make up answers to a child's question. If you are unsure about the answer, say you do not know. Children deserve honesty and they need for a trusted adult to be forthright and upfront with them.

- *Do not be surprised if your child reports to someone outside the family* — Children do not want to upset their parents, and they know that reporting sexual abuse will be upsetting. They also may be dealing with reporting that someone they and their parents know and trust abused them. In addition, they become concerned about parents' reactions and, as a result, they often seek the advice of someone they trust as they go through the initial disclosure.

Ultimately, the goal is to encourage children to speak up. Learning to deal with those disclosures will help create an environment that provides children with the freedom to speak up and tell someone if anyone touches them inappropriately. Encourage communication and openness in talking with children. Let them know they can tell you anything — and they will!

Do not limit the discussion to young children, or decide you no longer need to keep talking about it with older teens. The need to teach and reinforce the message about the potential risks of sexual abuse never ends. As children grow older, there are other messages parents must share.

For example, teens need to know about the possibility that predators could be posing as modeling agents or photographers as a way to lure them into compromising situations. They also need to know about date rape drugs and how to protect themselves at parties and special events. They need to be reminded that there is no place in any relationships, particularly those that are supposed to be based on love and care, for violence, forcing people to perform sexual acts, or threats of abandonment if sexual favors are not performed.

Parents need to reinforce the message over and over. Be aware of teachable moments, and take advantage of the opportunity to educate young people and raise awareness about the cunning and creative skills and abilities employed by sexual predators in the grooming process. Young people, particularly older teens, may think they can outsmart a predator. Parents and other caring adults must continually reinforce the need for heightened awareness and skepticism when someone's behavior raises concerns of any kind. Arrogance about what they think they know about how to protect themselves can backfire on teens. The generosity and openness of young teens is no match for the skill and cunning of a sexual predator.

If children are participating in activities that may leave them vulnerable or could lead to risky circumstances, remind them of the rules and the fact that you are there for them anytime. They may seem irritated that you are bringing the issue up again, but it is much better to deal with their annoyance than to counsel a child recovering from a sexual assault or a betrayal of trust.

In addition to maintaining communication with your children, remember to develop relationships with their friends. Let them know you are there to listen and support and create a safe space for other children and teens to speak up.

Paying attention to the conversations that take place in your presence can be an eye opening and valuable experience. Parents sometimes talk about the value of "car talk." They offer to provide transportation to young teens and pay close attention to the conversations that take place during the trip. If the current buzz words leave you confused as to what the conversation is about, an Internet search for "teen slang" can help you decipher the conversations and learn more about your child's interests and activities.

Being alert to all that is happening in your child's life is the best way to recognize the potential vulnerabilities and address the risks. Pay attention to the clues about what is going on in the life of your children. Listen to what they say. Listen to their friends. Pay attention to what's important to them. Know what they are saying online. Be aware of the joys and the challenges that your child is dealing with every day. Then you will have the information to provide them with the tools they need to be your partner in promoting their safety.

CHAPTER 25

How to Know a Sex Offender is Now Safe

The axiom at the heart of all *Arpeggias*® materials is: "There is no cure for pedophilia. Prevention is the only cure." Successful treatment is possible, but no one has found a "cure" for these sexual disorders. In fact, it is unrealistic to believe that we will ever know whether a sex offender or sexual predator is "safe" to be around. If you think about it, the only way to find out for sure whether any predator is safe is to leave them alone with children who are attractive to them and see what happens. Who in their right mind would ever do that? So, the answer to the question, "How do we know when a sex offender is now safe?" is, "Never," and responsible adults should never assume that someone who molested a child is now safe for children to be with alone.

We need to remain alert to the risky situations, locations, and people in our children's lives and always have our attention on the behavioral warning signs of potential predators. Interrupting adult/child interactions when we see these behaviors is key to preventing abuse, whether the offender is known or unknown to us. Maintaining a "healthy suspicion" about every adult who interacts with children is our best defense against any risky adult, whether we know the person is a sex offender or not. Observing the interactions between adults and children is the responsibility of every adult in the environment. Interrupting situations that raise concerns is the right thing to do for everyone involved.

That point of view seems easier to advocate vigorously for when the sex offender is someone unknown to us personally. We can stand up firmly for what we believe is the right thing when the adult involved lives in someone else's neighborhood and comes in contact with someone else's children. But what about those predators who are part of our family or live in our neighborhoods, or the ones whose children attend school with our children?

How do we keep caring for and loving the members of our family who are dealing with this issue in their own lives?

How do we keep children safe from the devastating, destructive desires of others we love?

How do we love and support parents, siblings, and children who suddenly discover someone they love and trust is guilty of enormous betrayal?

There is an old saying that reminds families and friends it is "okay to love an alcoholic." The same could be said for the sexual predators who are part of our family. However, the problem is not, and never has been, "loving them." The problem is we somehow think that loving them means we must either enable or ignore their destructive behavior. It is fine to love or care for someone who commits this crime. It is inexcusable, however, to ignore what they do or make excuses for their behavior, and criminally irresponsible to fail to take every possible step to protect children (all children) from the risk of being abused. Loving a child molester simply means we accept that they do these things. We do not ignore it. We do not condone it. We do not make excuses for it, and we do not enable it or deny it either. In fact, we make sure we manage the environments when our loved one is around to ensure there is no opportunity for abuse to occur.

This does not mean members of the family should be shunned or excluded from family gatherings or celebrations. It just means that, as responsible adults, we must keep our priorities straight. Children must be safe! Everything else is secondary to that commitment. This means creating rules for perpetrators about their attendance at and participation in family events, and enforcing the rules WITHOUT EX-CEPTION! For example, we never allow them to be alone with children or to touch them in any way that is inappropriate or could be an access to intimate touch. We create these rules and guidelines with the adult involved and with other members of the family so everyone is clear that safety is the priority.

We cannot allow ourselves to be duped into being convinced that a genuine apology is enough to overcome our resolve to protect children from predators, or give credence to assurances from a perpetrator about a desire to change. Our willing-ness to believe that adult family members ought to get a second chance undercuts our obligation to protect children from the risk of harm.

Priority number one must always be to keep children safe. When someone in our family has molested a child, they have permanently forfeited the privilege of ever enjoying the company of our children unchaperoned or unsupervised. No amount of therapy, remorse, or professed regret can undo the damage or reinstate the opportunity to spend time alone with children in the family, particularly children of a type the perpetrator is attracted to.

Perpetrators may use any number of techniques to encourage us to give up on our primary objective. They have been know to use threats, promises, enticement, sweet-talk, coaxing, and persuasion to convince adults to back off of a firm position about this issue. Adults must be careful to keep the focus on the safety of the children and give up any concern for the feelings of the adult or the other members of the family.

It is possible to love someone who has hurt a child this way, and also to establish and enforce strict rules about their participation in family events. In a way, you could say it is not only our obligation to our children but to the perpetrator, too. Enforcing strict rules that keep perpetrators away from children can also protect the perpetrator from their own inability to control their desires. In that case, the rules make a difference for everyone involved.

Through this process we learn how to create and maintain appropriate boundaries. We learn how to love someone with a problem we don't understand, cannot condone, and often are horrified by. We also teach others how to create safe environments in any situation no matter what the issue.

Ultimately, we learn how to establish and enforce rules that keep children safe from sexual predators without eliminating the fun, joy, and spontaneity of life. At the end of the day, that is what we all want.

CHAPTER 26

Turning the Tide of Child Sexual Abuse Prevention – the "Big Picture"

In the mid 1800s, the city of Chicago was working hard to find ways to improve on existing sewage systems so as to impact the loss of life due to typhoid fever, cholera, and dysentery. However, no matter what they did to improve or expand the existing system, people were still dying in record numbers.

In 1887, a small group of engineers created a unique and unorthodox response to the problem. With their leadership, Chicago undertook a bold new approach to this persistent problem. They set about reversing the flow of the Chicago River. Between 1887 and 1922, against enormous odds, they created a series of canals and artificial rivers and the flow of the river was reversed. When that was accomplished, the threat of cholera and typhoid was eliminated almost immediately.

It took courageous, insightful thinking to imagine and implement this amazing feat. It took a willingness to acknowledge the accomplishments that had already been made and still look for a different way. It took perseverance and diligence to accomplish the task in the face of tremendous odds against it. Most of all, it took commitment to the health of the people of Chicago, fanning the flames of passion that drove those who saw this innovative idea through to a successful completion in the face of uncertainty, misunderstanding, skepticism, and disbelief.

Child sexual abuse is also a serious public health issue. Like the diseases facing Chicago, we know a lot about how to impact the situation after it happens, but not a great deal about how to prevent it.

According to the US Department of Health and Human Services, Administration for Children and Families, in the year 2006, there were 885,245 reported cases of child mal-treatment in the United States, and 8.8 percent of those, or 78,120, involved sexual abuse. In addition, experts agree that sexual abuse is grossly underreported.

Far too many of our children are subjected to the sexual desires of the very adults who are responsible for their care. There are many powerful and effective tools in place to deal with the consequences of child sexual abuse and more are being developed every day. However, as was discovered in Chicago in the efforts to end dysentery, cholera and typhoid, no treatment or crisis response will ever prevent child sexual abuse. The only way to protect children from the conse-quences of being molested is to stop the molesters before they can prey on our children; in effect, to reverse the flow of the prevention river.

Traditional child sexual abuse education efforts are valuable and should be continued. However, adults still lack the tools to prevent child sexual abuse. A new approach to the problem is needed. This new approach must take an entirely different view of the situation.

This book is intended to lay the foundation for mounting an effort to turn the tide of prevention education in much the same way those forward-thinking engineers turned the current of the Chicago River. To accomplish that goal, we need to teach adults how to *prevent* child sexual abuse, not merely deal with it after the fact.

We know which behaviors are risky. Recognizing these behavioral signs makes a difference in many aspects of dealing with this issue, such as in efforts to understand why predators molest children. To date, it has not made a big difference to *prevention* efforts except as related to the expansion of children's programs.

For example, awareness of the risky actions of predators helped those working with children's programs expand their materials to include the specific things a child molester might do to gain a child's trust and attention. As a result, better, more effective programs were developed for children and more information was provided to teachers, medical professionals, law enforcement officials, and others about how to deal quickly and effectively with the consequences of child sexual abuse. Programs like the Committee for Children's *"Talking about Touching"* and the companion piece for parents, *"What Do I Say Now?"* incorporated information gathered through the analysis of the behavior of predators. Again, the emphasis was on building a better program to educate children about how to protect themselves from the advances of a predatory adult.

Conspicuously absent, however, are programs, methods, or vehicles for applying the information in a meaningful way to educate adults about how to prevent child sexual abuse.

The challenge of actually delivering the information in an effective way to adults is daunting. We must literally turn the tide of prevention education and take it in an entirely new direction.

The mere size of this challenge appears to have thwarted any effort to devise a program to educate adults. Children need to be part of the education and prevention process and they are easier to reach. They gather in schools across the country to participate in the programs offered as part of the regular curriculum.

Adults are more difficult. How do we provide information to adults in a way that gives them the tools they need to recognize the behavioral characteristics of potential child molesters and intervene before abuse occurs? Adults do not gather anywhere in a predictable or reliable way that is similar to children in school. Getting adults together to participate in a program that addresses this issue is a challenge that, to date, no one except the Roman Catholic Church in the United States has adequately addressed.

Educating adults how to recognize other risky adults in the environment and stop them before a child is molested is the only way to really prevent child sexual abuse and it requires an innovative approach as well as creative, engaging programming.

There are programs that educate adults in unique ways and provide them with the tools. Finding an effective delivery mechanism is the difficult part. Organizations such as Empowering Adults – Protecting Children, Inc., a non-profit organization located in Oklahoma, are investing their time, energy, and resources into pioneering this new effort to educate adults and to design and implement program delivery models that can be replicated in other states and communities.

The goal is to find ways to reach out and create opportunities for parents, friends, guardians, grandparents, and other responsible adults to learn how to prevent child sexual abuse.

If we are committed to making a significant impact on the incidence of child sexual abuse in the United States, we must teach adults how to prevent it from happening. They need to know what to watch for and how to interrupt situations that raise concerns.

There is no cure for child sexual abuse. Prevention is the only cure and the key to protecting our children from sexual predators.

It is time for adults to realize that it will take focus, intentionality, and commitment to stop sexual predators. It is time to do our job of

...keeping them safe from the evil in our midst.